TEACHING SCIENCE TO INFANTS

Romola Showell

Ward Lock Educational
1983

45797

WARD LOCK EDUCATIONAL CO., LTD.
47 MARYLEBONE LANE,
LONDON W1M 6AX

A member of the Ling Kee Group
LONDON · HONG KONG · TAIPEI

ISBN 0 7062 3847 8

First published 1979

Reprinted 1979; 1980; 1981; 1983

Printed by Topman Printing Press Ltd.

CONTENTS

1 INTRODUCTION

Science begins as soon as a child starts to look around at the world and see all the things that are there — trees, animals, cars, stones, bridges, fire — the list is endless. It should begin when he first realizes that water pours and that birds can fly!

At school it must start in the infant classes and should be continued all through the primary school so that he acquires a background of knowledge that will help later on, and which will be a source of permanent interest.

Infants love doing things, and science cannot fail to appeal to them if it is introduced in the right way. There is a wealth of ideas for the teacher, even in the most impoverished environment, and it is only necessary to adapt these ideas to your classroom situation and to the ability of your children. A young child cannot concentrate for long and is not capable of making reasoned conclusions, but he can be taught to observe accurately and to experiment for himself. Recording has to be unsophisticated, but science is well worth the trouble taken in planning and preparation, and the results will more than repay the teacher's efforts.

GENERAL NOTES

1 It is never too early to show a child how to look at the things around him.

2 Science is an exact study — even for the youngest children — so all work, however elementary, must have an aim and a reasonable outcome. For example, looking at the school rabbit: Why are we looking at it? What can we expect the children to see? One reason could be as part of a study on the ways in which animals move; another could be because we wanted to show children some of the characteristics of living organisms.

3 Although biology-based topics are the most popular there are many possible aspects of physical science which should be considered, e.g. looking at metals, wheels, plastics, solid and liquid things or making simple weather recordings.

4 However simple the information given to a child *it must be accurate*, and do not be afraid to use adult words. Use 'male' and 'female' not 'mummy hamster' and 'boy guinea pig'. Admit you do not know all the answers to the questions asked, but suggest that you and the children find out the answers together, in some way. Never underestimate a child's knowledge. Modern children are used to watching the television

and the amount of information retained, even by the youngest child, can be very surprising.

5 Science must be practical and it is very easy to find suitable biological specimens, to structure relevant experiments and to make project visits. Why show a child a picture of a Dragon Fly before you have shown him the Wasps and Houseflies that can be seen with little effort?

6 Limit information. A visit to a zoo is fun, but it is too overwhelming for the child to absorb as a whole. Back at school limit any work done to one small section — animal coverings, birds, colouring etc.

7 Always record in some way. The method will depend on the age and the ability of the child, but I feel that this is the most important aspect of science teaching at this age. It forms the basis for the accurate observation and interpretation which are an essential part of science in the secondary school. There are many ways of recording but whatever method is chosen, the child must be able to display or talk about his work to the teacher, the class or any suitable group.

a Discussion. This can be talking together about work done or things seen. Each child in a group should be able to contribute to it.
b Talking and using a tape recorder. Even the youngest children can be taught to use a tape recorder and will soon learn to make commentaries, however hesitant and limited.
c Paintings and drawings.
d Models and collage pictures.
e Writing — from a single word or sentence to a structured piece of prose or creative writing.
f Talk or demonstration given by a child or a group of children to another group.
g Taking photographs.
h Making scrap books.

Children's work can be made into class books, display panels, friezes, project exhibitions, personal folders, tape libraries etc. It hardly matters as long as the children know that you are taking their work seriously. With infant science it is possible for the brightest and the slowest children to contribute something of value to the class's work.

8 Use good reference books, but make sure that the children use these for additional information. Older children like to produce a 'nice' piece of work and will often copy out undigested paragraphs. Teach the children to find the books they want, and the way to use them. Because a child can read he does not, necessarily, know how to find his way round a reference book or how to use an index. Even the pre-reading child needs books, and there are many with excellent illustrations that can be used. Do not ignore adult books because the text is too difficult. They can serve to show children good, accurate pictures and will be useful reference books for the teacher (who needs to be able to find the names

of trees, insects etc).

9 Work cards can be used with the older child who can read, but they tend to limit the work that is being done. A child, intent on finishing his card, often loses the sense of discovery that should be inherent in infant work. If cards are used they should be made with a specific child or group in mind, they should be well made and well written, and they should be in the form of 'How to do it guides' rather than a list of questions. Work cards are undoubtedly helpful with a large class but the teacher should be aware of their limitations.

10 Plan topics beforehand so that books, apparatus etc are ready. The flow diagrams in this book should help with the planning. They give some indication of the possible ways in which any particular topic can develop and they can also be altered, afterwards, and kept as a record of work done.

This is a book of ideas. It presents a series of topics which could be used with infant and first-school children, and which are likely to interest them and to make them more aware of their surroundings. It cannot be exhaustive, but I hope it will help the teacher who feels that he, or she, has little science knowledge, or who has hesitated to introduce the subject to infants. I have only included topics which I know from personal experience to be successful, but there are many more which teachers can think of themselves, and which may be better for use in their situations. All I can hope is that this book will give them a basis on which to begin.

Apparatus used throughout can usually be found in the school or can be collected easily. There are just a few items which need to be bought specially, and I have tried to keep these to a minimum. I would consider such things as good hand-lenses to be essential and, if the money is available, I would have a binocular microscope. Even a five year old can manage this, and it opens up entirely new worlds when the child can see the scales from a Butterfly's wing or the teeming life in a spoonful of pondwater. A list of apparatus is included so that a 'Science Box' can be collected. I have not put down the more obvious things such as paper, card, crayons, paints and gum which can be found in any classroom.

At the end of each section there is a bibliography with suggestions for books for the children and for the teacher. (These are listed in my personal order of usefulness.) At the end of the book there is also an additional list of general books which the teacher may find useful for further reference. It is not easy to find good information books for infants. Too often the reading level is far higher than the interest level and publishers seem afraid of straightforward fact books for younger readers. Even the smallest scientist likes clear, realistic pictures and, of course, information should be accurate.

It is virtually impossible to avoid science with active, inquisitive youngsters around you — and many teachers have been teaching it for years without even realizing it.

Why does an umbrella keep you dry in the rain? Why are wheels round? Is there a goldfish in your classroom? How does it breathe? What does it eat? Do all fish look like this? Why don't knees bend backwards as well as forwards? Talk about it. Enjoy it. Science starts at the very beginning — so make it fascinating for the children you teach!

2 APPARATUS

The lists which follow give details of useful apparatus to have in the classroom for any science work.

Easily collected

String
Rubber bands
Modelling clay
Nails
Pieces of wood (all sizes)
Plastic bottles
Plastic pots
Saucers
Jam jars
Plastic bags
Metal foil
Milk straws
Adhesive tape
Tin lids
Balls — all sorts
Tins (If the tops have been removed with a rotary opener there are no sharp edges.)

Wire
Paper clips
Scissors
Plastic spoons
Boxes (all shapes and sizes)
Matchboxes
Corks
Pins
Thread
Housebricks
Screws
Garden canes
Wax crayons
Marbles
Toy cars
Plastic sweet jars (Most shops are delighted to get rid of these — they make ideal insect jars and tanks for water snails and tadpoles.)

Tools

Hammer
Pliers
Hand-fork and trowel

Hacksaw
Indoor watering can
Screwdriver

Purchased apparatus

Aquarium tanks (Several small plastic ones are better than one large one. A large tank full of water is immovable.)
Hand-lenses (Cheap plastic ones scratch easily and are soon useless.)
Balance with deep pans

Meccano (The plastic set is particularly useful.)
Plastic funnels and measures
Timers — simple sand timers, and one second-timer
Plastic tubing
Flower pots
Outdoor thermometer

Mirrors (Unbreakable plastic mirrors are obtainable.)
Plastic washing-up bowls

Useful apparatus

(Very nice to have, but in no way essential.)

Binocular microscope
Animal inspection cage
Mouse/hamster cage
Seed propagator — seed tray and propagator lid with ventilators

Other apparatus

Tape recorder
Slide viewers
Slide and film-strip projector
Garden-fork and spade

3 GROWING THINGS

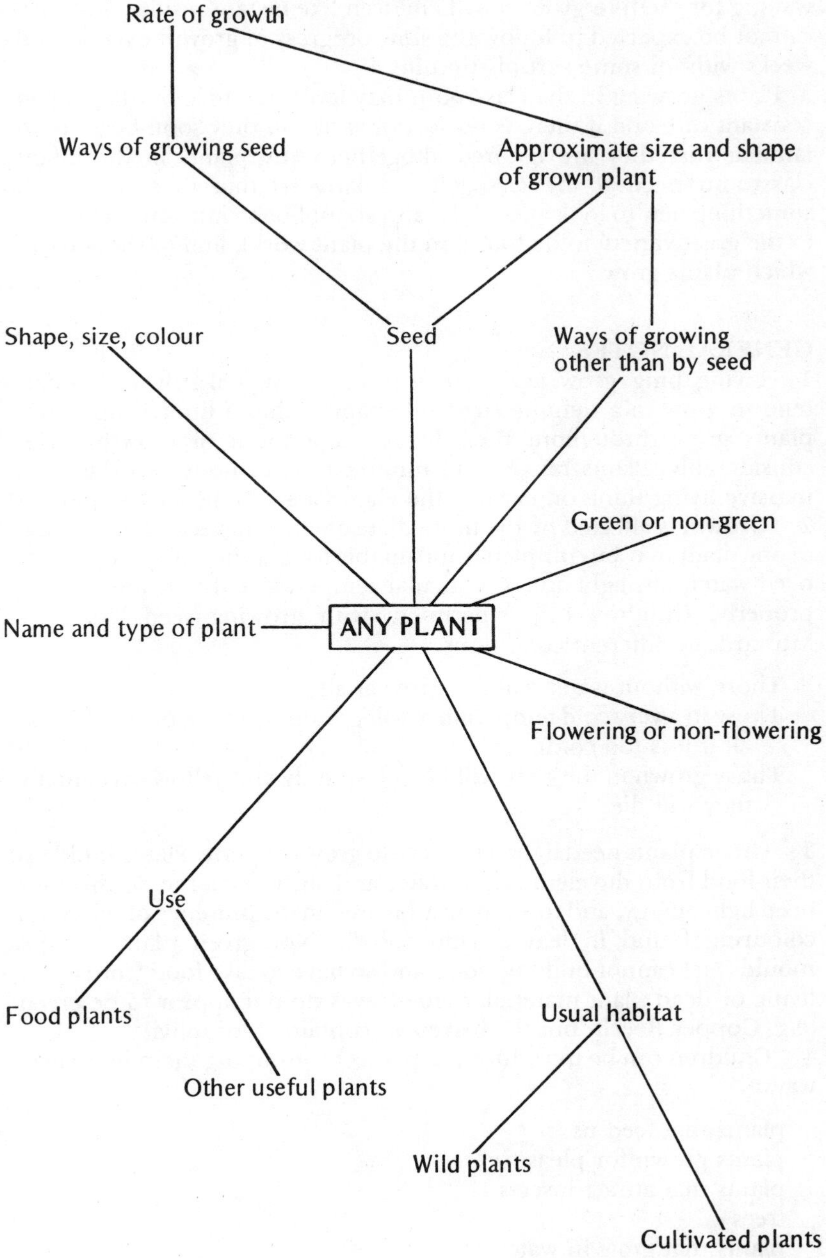

Growing plants will only be interesting for children if it is made interesting. Nothing is more boring than planting a few seeds and then waiting for them to grow. Small children like instant results, and they cannot be expected to follow the slow progress of growth over several weeks without some sort of stimulus.

Plants growing in the classroom may look very nice but they need constant care and if there is no sort of variation they soon become so familiar that they are ignored altogether. Any plants in the infant classroom need to be changed regularly so that there is always something new to look at, and the aim should be to introduce children to the great variety to be found in the plant world, and to the ways in which plants grow.

GENERAL NOTES

1 Living things grow, and increase in size is a sign of growth. Animals tend to grow to a definite size and shape within a limited time, but plants grow throughout their lives and amount of growth varies considerably. Plants range from minute to enormous and the most massive living thing on earth is the giant Coast Redwood (Sequoia).

2 Growth is affected by the immediate environment, and the habitat of one plant may be completely unsuitable for another. Basically plants need water, air, light and a particular temperature if they are to grow properly. Children can experiment with growing seeds, such as Mustard, in different conditions:

Those without water will not grow at all.
Those in a very cold temperature will grow only very slowly (or not at all if it is too cold).
Those grown in the dark will be tall, spindly and yellow. Eventually they will die.

3 Green plants need light if they are to grow properly. Plants build up their food from the elements in water and air. In order to do this they need light energy, and this can only be used in the presence of the green colouring found in leaves (chlorophyll). Non-green plants (fungi, moulds etc) cannot build up food and so have to take food from other living or dead plant material. Some leaves do not appear to be green (e.g. Copper Beech) but the leaves do contain chlorophyll.

4 Children can be introduced to plants by grouping them in various ways:

plants that feed us
plants grown for pleasure
plants that attract insects
trees
plants that grow in water
other useful plants — medicinal plants, Cotton and Flax, Teazles etc.

There are many other possible groupings and children can often suggest these for themselves.

5 Children tend to think that plants can only be grown from seeds, and this is the method of reproduction with which they are most familiar. They should be given the opportunity to look at a variety of seeds, and the larger seeds such as Pea and Bean can be soaked so that they can be pulled apart and the embryonic roots and shoots seen. Collections of seeds can be made quite easily so that children can see the difference in size, shape, colour and strength. Using a hand-lens would make this more interesting.

6 Many plants can also be grown vegetatively (that is, growth other than by seed). Common examples are:

bulbs and corms — Onion; Daffodil, Bluebell, Crocus
tubers — Potato, Dahlia
leaf and stem cuttings — Geranium, Mint
runners — Couch Grass, Strawberry.

Gardeners also use root division, by simply dividing up plants, and grafting (particularly Roses and fruit trees).

7 Other interesting features of plant growth which children could look at are:

climbing plants — the way in which stems spiral round other plants; tendrils clinging to hold the plant up; ways in which plants like ivy cling to trees and brickwork
the shape of plant roots
the variety of shape and colour in leaves
leaf-fall, in autumn
the movement of plants towards the light (leaves tend to grow towards light so that they can absorb the light energy for food building).

PLANNING AND PREPARATION

1 If young children are to grow seeds they should be involved from the start. They should prepare their own pots, plant the seeds, write the labels (unless still too young to do this) and should be shown how to care for them. If each child has his or her own pot then they are more likely to remain interested. Seeds can be grown in ordinary soil, or potting compost, in flower pots, yoghurt pots etc. For speedy growth Mustard is probably the best. The seeds can be scattered on the top of damp soil and will germinate in a day or two. Larger seeds can be grown singly, and experiments can be made with more unusual plants. Easy to grow are Mustard, Radish, Grass, Lettuce, Pea, Bean, Nasturtium, Castor oil and Tomato.

The children can also try some of the more interesting seeds like Maize, Wheat, Marrow, Cucumber, Peanut, Apple, Orange, Grapefruit, Acorn, 'conker', Dandelion, Bird seed, Onion and Carrot.

The hard seeds of Plums and Peaches, Dates and Avocados will grow but take a very long time to germinate.

2 Seeds can be planted in a variety of ways:

a On damp sawdust, cloth, blotting paper or sponge. Mustard is best for this but the dishes dry out very quickly and seedlings often die over the weekend in warm weather.

b In egg shells. If the shells are filled with soil and faces are painted on them, grass 'hair' can be grown.

c The old experiment of using a jam jar, lined with blotting paper and with a Pea or Bean seed pushed between the blotting paper and the glass is still very useful for showing the stages of growth. Little fingers soon tear damp blotting paper so fill in the space in the middle with sand, sawdust or cotton wool and do not water until the seeds are planted.

d Acorns and other larger seeds can be grown on the top of a bottle filled with water. Make sure that the water reaches the seed. Bulbs can be grown on the top of jars (an Onion will grow this way).

e Children can make 'mini-greenhouses' with a plastic bag and a rubber band. After the seeds have been planted in a flower pot, put a small plastic bag over the top (so that it sticks up to make a domed covering). Secure with a rubber band. If the soil is watered before this is done it should not need watering before the shoots appear. Water condensing on the bag will run down into the pot.

Mini-greenhouse

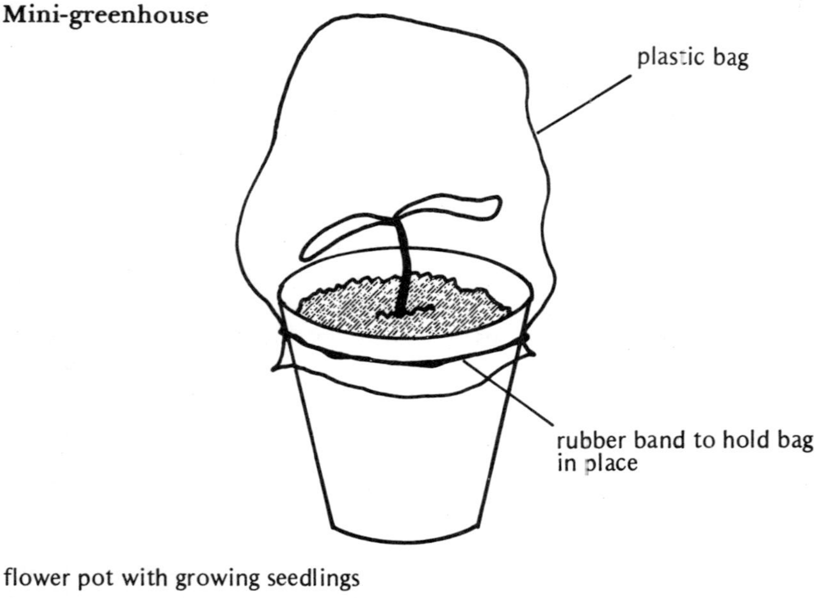

3 A plant's response to light can be shown using a healthy green plant in a pot, and a cardboard box with a lid (a shoe box will do for a small plant). Make a hole (about the size of a 50p piece) in the middle of one end of the box. Put the plant in the box, at the opposite end, and put on the lid. Keep the box in the same position with the hole facing a source of light. If the box is only opened for watering the leaves will bend towards the light hole. If a plant such as a Pea is used it can be left until the shoot eventually appears through the hole.

4 Give the children a reason for growing plants:

Grow Tomatoes and have a tomato-sandwich tea when there is enough fruit.

Grow Mustard and Cress in small pots and sell these, very cheaply, to the parents. Older children can work out cost and profit (or loss).

Grow Geraniums, Tradescantia etc from cuttings and sell these at the next school fair.

Offer to plant bulbs for other classes.

Grow tree seeds and plant the seedlings in the school garden, a child's garden etc.

5 Give children a chance to see plants they would not otherwise see — many city children are extremely ignorant about food plants. Grow Potatoes in large 12″ (30 cm) flower pots. One tuber will produce a reasonable number of potatoes and these can be seen to be growing on the tips of the underground stems, when the plant is dug up. The produce can be cooked and eaten! Grow Peas and Beans in large pots and keep them until the pods are formed; Cucumber plants will grow on a window sill and I have even seen a Vegetable marrow growing in a crowded reception classroom.

6 Make a collection of unusual plants (with the help of the children and their parents) but see that these are labelled and that they are not kept for too long. Cacti are interesting for a short time but they soon get dusty and neglected.

7 Quick results can be obtained from growing the tops of root vegetables. Cut the tops off carrots, parsnips or swedes and place them in saucers of water. Cuttings of Geranium also grow quickly, and sprigs of mint will produce roots if the bottom of the stems are stripped of leaves, and they are then left in water.

WORKING AND RECORDING

The youngest children can plant their seeds, and a class book could be made with the text depending on the age and ability of the children. If they provide the pictures the writing can be as brief as necessary: 'Today we planted the seeds.' 'The seeds were planted in pots.' 'The seeds need water.' 'Martin's seed has started to grow.'

Older ones can provide their own labels, details as to how they planted the seeds, and instructions for caring for them. Charts can be kept to show growth rate and drawings or paintings made to show different stages of growth. A 'plant show' could be held when all the plants are growing reasonably well, and certificates could be issued to the 'gardener of the week'.

If a variety of seeds are planted on the same day — by different groups of children — a germination and growth chart could be filled in:

Date the seeds were planted:			
Seed:	Date shoot appeared:	Number of days since planted:	Name of grower:

Plants growing in pots can have a strip of cardboard pushed into the side, and the height of the plant can be marked on this.

Children can make scrap books of plants in different categories (gardening catalogues are very useful for this), e.g. food plants, roots which we eat, cereals.

Having grown some of the possible plants older infants could see film-strips, look at pictures and read books to find out more about plants such as Cotton, Sugar Cane and Rice. This could serve as the basis for more concentrated topic work. They could also do some research work to answer specific questions about plants. These could be duplicated as enquiry sheets and the children could be given a definite time in which to try and find out the answers. If there are a number of poor readers in the class or group the questions could also be taped to help them with the reading, e.g.

Can you find the answers to some of these questions?
The largest plant in the world is a type of tree. Can you find out its name?
Some plants are not green. Can you think of a plant that is not green?
Some plants can be grown from bulbs. Can you find the name of a plant you can grow from a bulb?

What do you call plants that grow in the sea?

Some plants grow in fresh water. Can you find the name of one plant that grows in fresh water?

Weeds are plants, but they grow in gardens where we do not want them. Can you give the name of one weed?

Some plants have leaves we can eat. Can you name a plant with leaves that we eat?

A Christmas tree is a plant. Can you find out the real name of this tree?

SUPPORT MATERIAL

Books for the children

Plants and How They Grow F.E. Newing and R. Boxwood (Ladybird Books)

Plants B.J. Bampton (Macmillan)

The Seed Pamela Nash (Macmillan) (This is one of a set of six books in the 'See How it Grows' series)

Things that Grow Romola Showell (Ward Lock Educational)

Seeds and Weeds Starters Series (Macdonald Educational)

Learn about Indoor Gardening J. Griffin-King (Ladybird Books)

Books for teacher reference

Pocket Guide to Wild Flowers D. McClintock and R.S.R. Fitter (Collins)

A Field Guide to Mushrooms and Toadstools Morten Lange and F. Bayard Hora (Collins)

Early Experiences Science 5/13 (Macdonald Educational)

Introduction to Biology D.G. Mackean (John Murray)

Useful apparatus

Flower pots and small plastic pots; small trowels or old spoons; seed trays; packets of seeds (as many as possible); hand-lenses; plastic bags; rubber bands; potting compost or soil; old saucers; pieces of sponge; blotting paper; indoor watering can; shoe boxes; jam jars; small bottles.

4 SEE HOW THEY GROW

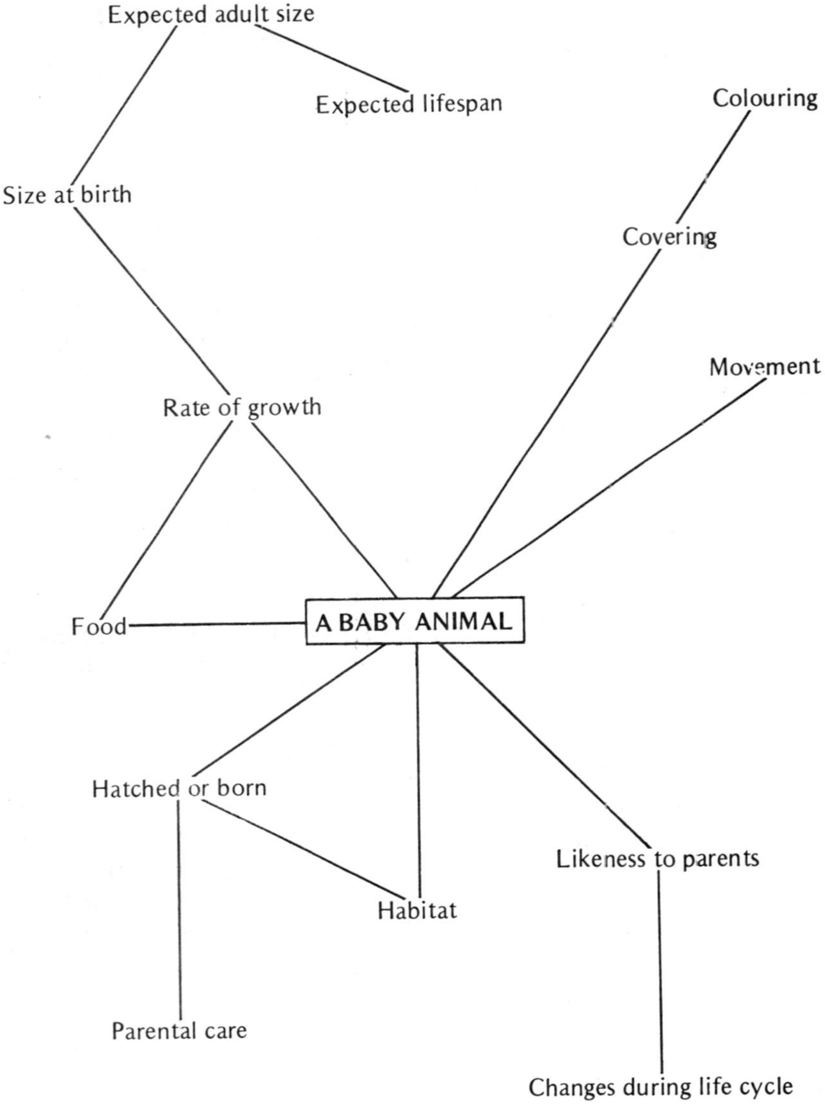

Note The term animal is used biologically to denote a living organism that is not a plant. The animal kingdom includes all the vertebrates, the insects and spiders, the worms, the molluscs, the crustaceans etc.

The attractions of a kitten, a puppy, a baby Guinea Pig or a human baby never fail with children. They are small, often playful and easy to handle. The lamb or calf seems infinitely preferable to the Sheep or Cow, and often infant children do not seem to associate the young animal with the adult. They accept that the kitten will eventually become a Cat, but do not seem to notice the stages in between; it is as if they were two completely different species, and that there is an instantaneous change at some point in time.

They accept, also, that they themselves grow but 'when I was a little baby' is something very remote, even for a five year old.

Infants can be introduced to the facts that growth and change are characteristics of living things, and that, in some cases, the changes can be so remarkable that the baby bears little resemblance to the adult (tadpole to Frog; caterpillar to Moth). Even the youngest child will realize that plants grow from seeds, and that baby birds hatch from eggs. They can be shown other eggs —Frog spawn and insect eggs — from which other animals hatch, and can be told that some baby animals (notably the mammals) grow inside the mother animal until they are ready to be born. Better still, they can share the excitement of waiting for the Guinea Pigs or Rabbits to be born.

Growth in animals is an interesting topic and the aim should be to show children the changes that occur during the growth and development from birth, or hatching, to adulthood.

GENERAL NOTES

1 Animals grow to a definite size and shape according to their species, so a Mouse will never grow as large as an Elephant, and a Cat will not have the neck of a Giraffe. Once the full size is reached (and the time taken to do this varies considerably) variations will be slight, depending basically on the food supply. Length of life varies also — Man being the longest living animal with a lifespan sometimes of over 100 years.

2 Animals need food for growth, energy and replacement of tissue. The natural food depends on the type of animal, but all animals — even the carnivores — depend on plants for food:

Food chains

Plankton→→→→Small Crustaceans→→→→Herring→→→Man
(plants)

Wheat seeds→→→→Field Mouse→→→→Owls

Grass→→→→→Rabbit→→→→→Fox

3 Baby mammals resemble the adults, and growth changes involve increase in size and weight, development of skin covering and changes in the teeth. Baby birds may not look exactly like the parent birds, but there is no doubt that they are birds. This does not apply to the young of

such animals as the Frog, Newt and many of the insects where the adult looks quite unlike the young animal.

4 The life cycle of the Frog will provide an example of an animal undergoing a complete change:

Egg →→→→→→→ Larval stage →→→→→→→→→→→→→Frog
(spawn) (tadpole) gradual change

Tadpoles are easy to keep in the classroom, but children should be taught conservation at an early age and they should be told that if they find frog spawn they should take only a few eggs. These are best kept in a small fish tank with the bottom covered with sand and small stones, and with a good supply of water weed set in small pots containing soil (the soil can be kept from dirtying the water if the surface is covered with sand or stones). If a tank is unavailable, two or three tadpoles can be kept in a jam jar or a plastic sweet bottle (but provided with sand and weed in the same way as the tank).

Mini-tank

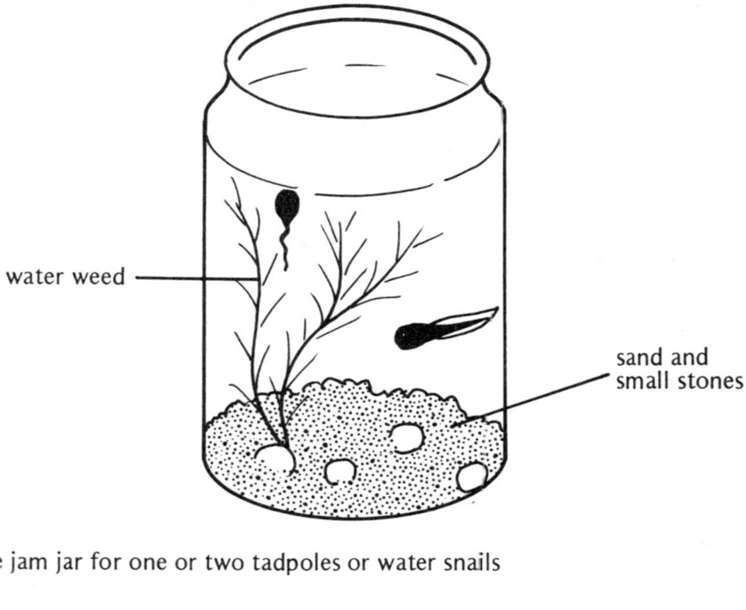

Large jam jar for one or two tadpoles or water snails

At first the tadpoles will feed on the jelly of the spawn, and then on the weed. They are vegetarian until their legs have grown, and when their back legs have appeared they will need a change of diet. A very small piece of raw meat can be attached to a thread and lowered into the tank for a short time (it must never be left in the tank) and the tadpoles will feed from this. As soon as the front legs grow the tadpoles need to be able to get out of the water. They can either have a floating raft or a large stone for this, and once they have completely changed they should be returned to the pond where the spawn was found. Frogs are very difficult to keep successfully in captivity. For a different life cycle see Section 8 *Insects*.

5 Guinea Pigs are ideal for small children to study because their babies can be handled carefully within a few hours of birth; they are born furred, their eyes are open and they will run around the cage when only one or two days old. Like all other pets they must be caged and cared for properly (see Section 10 on the care of small mammals), but they can be weighed and measured, and records kept of their food without any trouble.

6 When children use the word 'animal', they usually mean 'mammal'. Mammals are animals that produce milk for feeding their young, and in most cases eggs are not laid but the embryo is developed inside the body of the female. Animals born in nests — Rabbits, Mice, Hamsters, Hedgehogs etc —are quite helpless at birth and need to be cared for by the parent for some time. Other mammals — like Cows, Horse, Deer and Sheep — are born outside and have a covering of hair. They can move about almost immediately.

PLANNING AND PREPARATION

1 The children can see a young mammal with its mother — a kitten, a puppy, a calf, baby Gerbils, Mice, Hamsters or Rabbits. They can discuss the differences and similarities between the two animals, and can decide how much the baby will have to grow before it is as big as its mother. Colouring often interests children and they are puzzled as to why a kitten should be, say, black while its mother is a tabby. This will give an opportunity of talking about the father and the part played by the male in the development of the young. Human babies should not be forgotten, and it may be possible to persuade one of the mothers to bring her new baby into the classroom for the children to see.

2 Plan a visit to a farm or a zoo in the spring when there are likely to be young animals. Look at birds, fish and reptiles as well as mammals. If the children see birds, show them the structure of a bird's egg. This can be done easily using an ordinary hen's egg.

3 Keep tadpoles, caterpillars, Water Snails, Snails, Stick Insects etc so that the children can watch the changes as they grow. They can record these changes with pictures, written work or models.

4 Use slides and film-strips to show:

young animals and adult animals
variation in size and colour in the animal kingdom
the great variety of species in the animal kingdom
animals in their natural habitat.

5 Keep a pair of small mammals for breeding. The most suitable for infants are Guinea Pigs. Others recommended are Rabbits and Mice. Hamsters and Gerbils can bite and should not be handled at all by young children. Gerbils will also kill any strange animals introduced into their cage (with very unpleasant and messy results).

The children should be taught to care for the animals themselves (under supervision), to handle them properly, to measure out the correct amounts of food and to see that other children treat them with equal care. It needs to be remembered, however, that these animals will need looking after during weekends and school holidays, and provision will have to be made for this.

6 If possible get one or two baby Chickens or Ducks (but make sure that you have somewhere to take them when they have become too big for the classroom). A local secondary school may have an incubator where the children could watch chicks hatching from the eggs, or a local farmer may be willing to 'lend' a few chicks to a school for a short time.

7 If you have access to a baby animal the children can weigh and measure it regularly. Measure length from the tip of the nose to the end of the tail — not easy with a wriggling animal. Small animals (like Mice) can be weighed in scales with a deep pan or put into a paper bag for a few moments. Larger animals are more difficult. E.J. Arnold supply a balance with a bucket at each side which can be used for some, but it may be necessary to weigh a child, and then let it stand on the scales holding a larger animal (such as a Dog) and subtract the child's weight from the total weight to find out how heavy the Dog is.

Weight charts can be kept:

Guinea Pig Born May 11	May 12	May 15	May 18	May 21	May 24	May 27
Weight						
Length						

8 Very young children find the comparison of size difficult, so that 'very small' may mean anything from an Ant to a foal, and 'very big' usually means anything bigger than themselves. It is better to collect pictures and to make a frieze putting animals in order of size, e.g.

Ant→Bee→Snail→Sparrow→Hedgehog→Rabbit→Hen→Dog→Sheep
↓
Blue Whale←Elephant←Hippopotamus←Rhinoceros←Carthorse←Cow

Children seem to worry very little about pictures being to scale (and it will probably be impossible to have pictures all to one scale unless you happen to be an artist yourself). Pictures of a Mouse and an Elephant, both apparently of the same size are unlikely to muddle them. They accept that the one is small enough to hold, and the other is as 'big as a bus'.

WORKING AND RECORDING

Work with animals can go on at any time, and if animals are kept in school they will always be available for children to see. Whatever animals are kept — from Woodlice to Rabbits or Chickens — the children can watch them, talk about them, write about them, draw them, model them and learn to care for them. They will need constant reinforcement if they are to remain interested, and they will not learn anything from a Rabbit kept in a cage (however well looked after) if it is never taken out for them to touch, and if they are not given the chance to talk about it. Have they really noticed that it has long ears and a very small tail? What are its teeth like? Rabbits are gnawing animals and they have teeth that grow constantly; can the children think why this is important?

They can make books using their own drawings or cut-out pictures, e.g.

Very Small and Very Big Animals
Baby Animals
Farm Animals and Their Babies
Animal Records (The largest animal, the fastest animal, the smallest mammal, the largest insect etc.)

They can make books of work done by the class, e.g.

The Story of the Frog
A Book about Mice
All about Our Chickens
Snails.

Older children can make instruction cards, e.g.

Looking after the Tadpoles
How to Weigh the Rabbit
Caring for Your Cat
Feeding Gerbils.

Older infants can try to find the answers to various problems set for them, e.g.

1 A Mouse eats half its own weight in food every day. Could you do that? Would you need that much food? (The children can weigh one of their group, and can then weigh out food, half the child's weight, and see what it looks like.)

2 Some animals eat meat, some eat vegetables and some eat both. Do all large animals eat meat?

3 Can you find out how long it is before these animals are fully grown? Approximately how long will they live (if they are not killed)?

Name	*Fully grown at*	*Life span*
Cat		
Cow		
Mouse		
Man		
Butterfly		
Elephant		
Sparrow		
Duck		
Frog		
Goldfish		
Tortoise		

SUPPORT MATERIAL

Books for the children

Growing Up B.J. Bampton (Macmillan)
My Puppy is Born Joanna Crole (Lutterworth Press)
Living Things Romola Showell (Ladybird Books)
Our Bird Friends Jean Wilson (W. & R. Chambers) (Set of 6 small books)
Animals of Warmer Lands Jean Wilson (W. & R. Chambers) (Set of 6 small books)
Animals in Spring Vera Croxford (Transworld)
Frogs Starters Series (Macdonald Educational)
Very Small Animals Starters Series (Macdonald Educational)
Baby Animals John Leigh-Pemberton (Ladybird Books)

Books for teacher reference

Animals and How They Live F.E. Newing and R. Bigwood (Ladybird Books)
Science from the Beginning (Book 1) B.L. Hampson and K.C. Evans (Oliver and Boyd)
A Field Guide to the Mammals of Britain and Europe F.H. Van Den Brink (Collins)
The Oxford Book of Invertebrates David Nichols and John Cooke (OUP)

Useful apparatus:

Plastic sweet jars, jam jars etc covered with a piece of material cut from tights or stockings make suitable containers for a few caterpillars;

suitable animal cages; balances with deep pans; personal scales; tape measures; hand-lenses; camera; equipment for cleaning out animal cages (small shovel, scraper, bucket).

5 ALL SORTS OF GARDENS

terms of the type

$$(B^{-1}B_{-i})(B^{-1}B_{-j}) \dots (B^{-1}B_{-e})B^{-1} \qquad (i, j, \dots, e = 1, \dots, s)$$

can be approximated to zero. This would reduce the number of parameters to be estimated.

The results obtained are independent of the weights originally introduced. This is due both to the definition of the loss-function and to the linearity of the model. Consequently, at least in this linear hypothesis, another weighting system should be considered.

The important feature of the analysis is the generality of the approach and more specifically the integration of 'lagged variables' into the class of endogenous variables proper. Only two sets of variables remain, the exogenous and endogenous variables, and this dichotomy is preserved throughout.

5 Conclusions

These can be brief.

The history of urban dynamics will in fact be the same as that of national dynamics. So far, propositions have been generated by simple dynamic models (Schouten, 1967), more complex models have been simulated (Holland and Gillespie, 1963), and interdependent non-linear dynamic models have now been simulated and run under alternative policy conditions (de Biolley and Paelinck, 1970).

The general trend is clear and it now remains to be realized—and efforts are underway to prove the pudding by the act of eating. Optimistically our next paper on the subject will be a progress report.

References

Ancot, J. P., Paelinck, J. H. P., 1970, "A proposal for the estimation of parameters of simultaneous nonlinear equations systems", Faculty of Economics, Laboratory for Mathematical Economics, Econometrics and Operations Research, Namur, Working Papers No.3.

de Biolley, T., Paelinck, J. H. P., 1970, "Un modèle dynamique pour l'économie Belge: simulation et optimisation", *Optimisation et Simulation de Macro-Décisions: Recherches Théoriques et Appliquées*, Econometric Series, **3**, Laboratory for Mathematical Economics, Econometrics and Operations Research, Faculty of Economics, Namur.

Holland, E. P., Gillespie, R. W., 1963, *Experiments on a Simulated Underdeveloped Economy* (MIT Press, Cambridge, Mass.).

Jaumotte, C., Paelinck, J. H. P., avec la collaboration de Leheureux J. M., Pietquin, M., 1969, *Un Modèle de Simulation Dynamique pour une Région Urbaine,* Recherches Economiques de Louvain, **5**, 371-400.

Marquardt, D. L., 1963, *Journal of Industrial and Applied Mathematics,* **6**, 431-446.

Paelinck, J. H. P., 1970, "Some dynamic urban growth models", Papers of the Regional Science Association (Copenhagen Conference, 1969), **24**, Philadelphia.

Schouten, D. B. J., 1967, *Dynamische Macroeconomie*, 2 volumes (Stenfert-Kroese, Leiden).

Equilibrium versus Optimum: Spacing of Firms, and Patterns of Market Areas†

M.J.BECKMANN
Brown University, Providence, Rhode Island, USA

Introduction

Problems of optimum location are very much under discussion again (Mills and Lav, 1964; Bos, 1965; Beckmann, 1968; Schärlig, 1969; Serck-Hanssen, 1970). There has not been such interest in this topic since the pioneering work of Christaller (1966) and Lösch (1964). The purpose of this paper is to clarify, through direct calculations, what happens in a homogeneous market of one and two dimensions when markets are liberalized from a single firm monopoly to multiple firm monopoly to free entry; and to demonstrate how the market falls short of welfare maximization. At the same time we shall solve some of the mysteries that have surrounded the shapes of market areas under free entry in a two-dimensional economy. We shall limit ourselves to mill pricing for reasons that will become apparent in the course of the analysis. The reader is invited to extend the calculations to the cases of uniform, and perfectly discriminating, market prices.

1 One-dimensional model

Let firms be spaced at equal distances $D = 2R$. Following tradition assume that population density is uniform and that demand functions are linear and the same everywhere.

$$q = a - bp ,$$

where q is the quantity demanded, p is the price, and $a, b > 0$ are parameters of the demand function.

Also let each firm have the same fixed cost F and the same constant marginal cost c. Let transportation cost be proportional to amount and distance, and equal to k for sending one unit of the commodity over a unit distance.

† Research Papers in Theoretical and Mathematical Economics under NSF Grant #2325.

Watching things grow can be fascinating for both adults and children, and making gardens of all sorts can be a very worthwhile project for infant classes. Obviously a school with plenty of ground where a class can have its own strip of garden has a much easier task, but gardening can be carried out anywhere, however unlikely the school environment.

To keep young children interested over the weeks necessary for any plants to grow, the gardens need to have some feature that makes them special and individual participation is much more likely to lead to a continual awareness of what is going on. If you do all the work and then expect the children, day after day, to go and look at your garden then you are going to be disappointed. They want something of their own.

For children brought up in districts without gardens the idea of caring for plants seems strange. Plants are merely things that grow in the park or 'in the country', and they have little idea of planting, watering, weeding, harvesting etc. Children who are used to seeing growing things around them every day often ignore the familiar, and though they may be quite knowledgeable about particular plants, they are probably not aware of such things as the life cycle of plants, their importance as food, and the necessity of favourable conditions if they are to grow properly.

Gardening, however simple and however small scale, can introduce children to the pleasure of growing things, to the economic significance of plants and to some of the basic necessities for healthy growth.

GENERAL NOTES

1 Indoor gardens

a *Bowl gardens* Miniature gardens can be made in plastic washing-up bowls, an old sink or an old baby bath. The bottom must be lined with small stones to assist drainage, and ideally the bowl should be filled up with potting compost, but if this proves too expensive (and quite a lot is needed if several groups of children are making gardens) use sieved garden soil instead. You will get weeds growing, but this will help to make the mini-gardens more realistic! Plan the bowl as if it was a real garden and decide on suitable small plants. Grass seed can be sown to make a lawn, and when this has grown it can be kept trimmed with scissors. The seeds of small plants, such as Alyssum and Lobelia, can be planted to make borders, or small rockery plants can be used and trees can be seedlings of Sycamore or Oak, or any others that the children may have grown in pots. Not only plants but special features can be added. A margarine pot sunk into the soil will make a pond, and a few pieces of water weed can be put in this with one or two very small Water Snails; a path can be made from small flat stones; fences can be made from ice-lolly sticks, and a house could be built from one of the various building kits.

b *Bottle gardens* A narrow-necked bottle is too difficult for little children to plant, and as it is unlikely that they will be able to achieve the perfect bottle garden (which requires very little attention) it is useful to use a container that is big enough to weed or to snip off bits of fast growing plants. Use any glass jar with a wide neck and a lid — a large jam jar, a sweet jar laid on its side, a goldfish bowl with a metal foil lid or a glass kitchen storage jar. Put some small stones in the bottom, and then potting compost mixed with a little charcoal (but if this is unavailable use garden soil instead). It is not easy to establish a really successful bottle garden, but children like doing this and it probably does not matter that it will not last too long. Suitable plants are small ferns, and small-leaved ivies, but let the children experiment with any small plants that they want to grow. Some pleasant, short-term results can be achieved quite easily, and the gardens will last for some weeks. Once planted and watered the lid should be put on the container, and it should not need watering again. Moisture collecting on the side will run back into the soil. The plants need plenty of light, but do not put the garden in full sunlight or so much moisture will condense on the sides that it is impossible to see inside.

c *Water gardens* A goldfish bowl can be used to make a small water garden. Washed sand can be put in the bottom and the plants anchored with small stones. Plants can be bought from pet shops or garden centres dealing in aquatics, or plants can be collected from a pool or stream. A few Water Snails will help to keep the sides of the bowl free from algae, but not too many, because they feed on water plants.

d *Mould gardens* Moulds are fungi and included in the plant kingdom, but they do not contain the green colouring (chlorophyll) necessary for the building up of plant food. They must obtain their food from dead or decaying materials such as stale, damp foodstuffs. Moulds can be grown by placing moistened stale bread, orange peel, apple skin, cake etc in a plastic box covered with a lid. If this is kept somewhere warm the moulds will begin to appear in a few days. If the children can look at these with a good hand-lens or a binocular microscope they can see something of the structure. The feeding and reproduction of the moulds is too complicated to explain at this stage, but children enjoy an opportunity to see these unusual plants.

2 Outdoor gardens

A garden can be made in any corner of a playground. Part of the children's project can be the building of a small wall to enclose it. The wall can be built out of housebricks either left loose or cemented together (pre-packed bags of sand and cement mixture are obtainable from ironmongers and Do-It-Yourself stores). This garden can be filled with soil and used to plant Peas, Runner Beans, Radishes, Lettuce, herbs or a Vegetable Marrow. Children can be intoduced to the idea of adding fertilizer to the soil to improve growth. Use any general purpose fertilizer (such as Growmore) and use it according to the directions on the packet. These corner gardens also make ideal rockery gardens.

Boxes and large flower pots can be used for outdoor gardens. The size of the boxes will depend on what is available but they should be strong, and raised off the ground on tiles or bricks to help drainage. These should be treated like any small garden plot, but should not be placed where there will be a constant dripping of water, or where they are so sheltered that they will get insufficient light and water. These can be purely decorative, but let the children choose the plants. They can be shown a seed catalogue (where you have marked suitable plants) or they can bring seeds or plants from home. These boxes and pots can be used for bulbs in the spring and a mixed collection is preferable to a tasteful arrangement of Tulips, Hyacinths etc. On the whole small children seem to prefer growing vegetables and, providing the plants are not overcrowded, most vegetables can be attempted.

A garden plot is ideal because of the greater scope, but this also needs careful planning. The plot can be divided into strips so that each group of children has its own area, or plants can be grown under varying conditions. The latter is probably better for older children. They can, say, grow rows of Peas; one row can have a chemical fertilizer, one compost or manure, one could be watered regularly, one never watered, one could be left overcrowded etc and growth and yield can then be compared. The plot can be made into a specialized garden — a herb garden, a garden of sweet-smelling plants, a blue-flower garden, a garden of tree seedlings etc. There are numerous possibilities. It can also be used to make a wild garden, particularly in an area where children have little opportunity to see plants growing naturally. Part of the experiment can be to see just what will grow successfully on the soil in your district, and it may be possible to attract insects (e.g. nettles will attract the Small Tortoiseshell Butterfly).

PLANNING AND PREPARATION

1 Having decided which types of gardens it will be possible to attempt, you will have to collect together the necessary materials. If children are going to plant indoors, some large sheets of polythene are a useful way of protecting table tops. They can make a great deal of mess sieving soil and any large bowls and trays will make the job easier. Small trowels will be needed for planting, but old spoons will do just as well.

2 Discuss the gardens with the children and make use of their ideas. It is far better for them to experiment than to be told that your way is better. Plants that have died because they were not watered have provided a lesson in themselves, and the reasons for the plants dying can be discussed.

3 Provide a collection of labels for the names of the seeds planted, and for the names of the children planting them. These will need to be fairly substantial, e.g. ice-lolly sticks which can be written on in pencil.

4 If the children are going to grow vegetables give them a purpose for

growing them, e.g.

Bunches of radishes can be taken thome or sold to the parents, and other children. The same can be done with Lettuce, and Mustard and Cress.
Indoor gardens can be displayed somewhere in the school, with the names of the gardeners.
Tree seedlings can be replanted somewhere suitable, and can serve as a lesson in conservation.
Potatoes, Peas, Beans etc can be cooked and eaten by the class.
Counts can be taken of the insects visiting flowers.

5 If the children are going to use an outdoor plot and it needs digging, try and get older children to help with this if you are dealing with four or five year olds. Older infants will be able to manage (unless the ground is exceptionally overgrown or heavy) if they have good hand-forks.

WORKING AND RECORDING

Children who can read can be given instruction cards telling them what to do if they are making something specific such as a bottle garden:

Making a Bottle Garden
Wash out your jar or bottle and dry it.
Put some small stones in the bottom.
Put about 7 cm of soil on top of the stones. Use the soil labelled 'bottle-gardens' from the table.
Make the soil level but do not push it down too hard.
Use a spoon to put in the plants you have chosen.
See that the roots are covered.
Water carefully so that the soil is damp. Do not get it very wet.
Put on the lid, and put your bottle in the light.
Get a label, write on it your name, the names of the plants and the day you planted your garden.

Instructions will need to be written for each particular project.

Children can keep records of their planting, the progress of their plants and the results of the planting. The younger children can draw their gardens, they can tell you about them and they can tell other children about them. Older ones can make small books telling the story of their gardens, or they can write a class gardening book of instructions for making a garden.

Records can be kept of the cost of each particular project, and if the vegetables etc are sold, the children can work out if they have made a profit or loss.

Scrap books can be made using seed and plant catalogues, and seed packets.

The children could visit a greenhouse to see the plants growing there and could discuss the advantages of growing plants in greenhouses and frames.

Photographs could be taken of the gardens made, and it might be possible to hold a class 'Flower Show'. Older children could decide on categories of entries and could make simple entry forms, e.g.

The best pot of Mustard and Cress
The largest Radish
The best bottle garden
The best collection of flowers.

They could also make the certificates for the prizewinners.

SUPPORT MATERIAL

Books for the children

Learn about Indoor Gardening J. Griffin-King (Ladybird Books, also useful for the teacher)
Seeds and Weeds Starters Series (Macdonald Educational)
Look at Flowers Starters Series (Macdonald Educational)
Crops We Grow R.H.C. Fice and I.M. Simkiss (E.J. Arnold)

Books for teacher reference

Tackling Problems (Part 1) Science 5/13 (Macdonald Educational)
Wild Flowers of Verges and Waste Land Jean Imrie (A. & C. Black)
The Puffin Book of Gardening Mary Kelly (Penguin Books)
Any basic gardening book.

Useful apparatus

Plastic bowls and trays; flower pots; hand-trowels and forks; spoons; potting compost; packets of fertilizer; stones; garden canes; labels; hand-lenses; sweet jars; large glass jars; goldfish bowls; packets of seeds.
Note Whilst glass jars and goldfish bowls are very suitable for indoor gardening, for safety reasons small children should not carry these about. They are very heavy when full of soil or water.

6 A LOOK AT SOIL

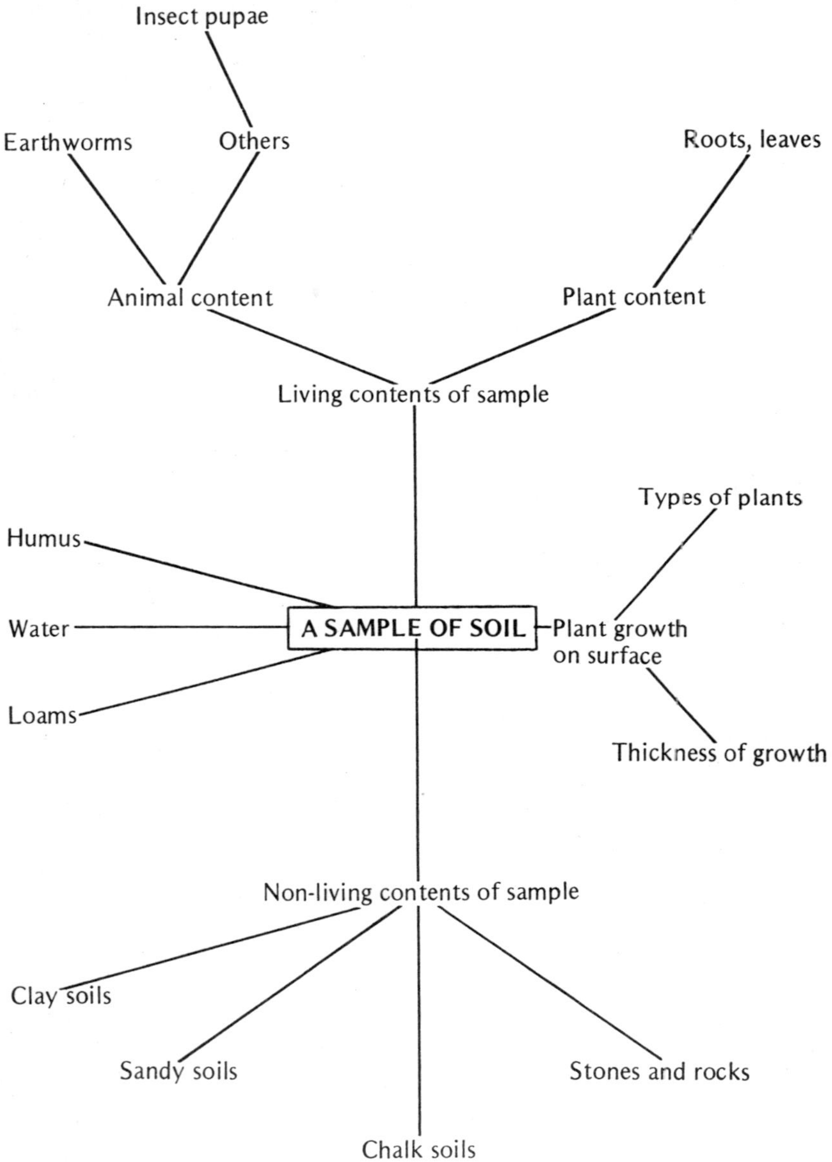

Soils in specific areas Salt marshes, pine woods, stream beds, cliffs etc can all be looked at if they are available.

If children have been planting seeds or making gardens they have, almost certainly, been using soil. The town child's attitude towards it can be seen by his almost indiscriminate use of the word 'dirt' instead of the word 'soil', and even the older child, used to seeing planting, growing and harvesting, often does not realize how much soils can vary.

Most young children take great pleasure in digging and playing about with soil. While they have been digging holes they may have noticed roots, worms and pieces of decaying leaves, and may have found that there are stones which sink to the bottom when they make mud.

They may have the opportunity to see earth-moving machinery at work, and to see how the layers vary from the top vegetation to the lower, sandy areas. However children are introduced to this particular topic they should, in the end, have some idea of the importance of soil as a growing medium for plants and how its fertility affects us all.

GENERAL NOTES

1 Soil is not a living material, but consists of particles of rock broken down by the action of water, heat and plant growth. Sub-soil contains very little humus (decayed plant and animal material). Top soil is generally darker because of the humus in it. Soil contains sand, clay, stones, mineral salts, humus, bacteria, water and air. It provides the growing medium for plants — air, water, food materials, anchorage and protection for seeds and roots.

2 Soils vary considerably. Sandy soils are warm, loose, full of air spaces and are easily worked. They are well drained but do not retain sufficient water during dry spells.

Clay soils are cold, heavy to work, and contain few air spaces. Because the particles are packed close together they become waterlogged. They contain more mineral salts than sandy soils.

Loam is a mixture of clay, sand and humus.

Chalky soils are greyish in colour, and have a characteristic plant growth, as there are many plants which cannot tolerate the excessive amount of lime in chalk soil.

3 Soil constantly flooded by the sea contains too much salt (sodium chloride) for most plants. Plants growing in salt marsh areas cannot absorb water in this concentrated solution of salt, so they only take in water during times of heavy rain, and are capable of storing this water within themselves.

4 If you cut into soil the different layers can be seen. The depth of each will vary in different areas. The top soil is darker, contains humus, and worms and insects live in it. The sub-soil is usually lighter in colour and firmer in texture; there are no Earthworms etc and the roots of the smaller surface plants do not penetrate the sub-soil. The bedrock may be of solid rock, or it may consist of broken, weathered rock on top of the solid rock.

5 There are many living organisms found in soil. As well as bacteria, protozoa, moulds and fungi there are numerous animals. These include Eelworms, Mites, Millipedes, Centipedes, insect larvae, Earthworms, Ants, Slugs and Beetles. Some feed on decaying plant and animal material, some feed on roots of growing plants and some prey on each other. The Earthworm is the most obvious animal for young children to study. It lives entirely in the soil, and feeds off the decaying plant matter in the soil that passes through its intestine. Many books recommend making wormeries but, apart from the actual construction, these provide very little of interest. The Worms soon disappear out of sight, and unless the box is kept properly damped they will soon die. It is far better to collect some large Worms, and to let the children see them. They can put the Worms on paper and hear them moving (the underside of the Worm has hair-like projections which catch on the paper); they can watch the muscular way in which Worms move and they can watch while they bury themselves into soft soil.

6 There are other animals associated with soil. Moles live largely in burrows in the soil, and their staple diet is Earthworms and caterpillars. They eat an enormous quantity of these and almost the whole of their lives is spent hunting for food.

Rabbits and Foxes make their burrows in soil and the young are born in these burrows.

The larvae of all the Hawk Moths (e.g. Lime Hawk, Poplar Hawk) pupate in soil.

PLANNING AND PREPARATION

1 Start any work on soil by letting the children look at and handle a sample of soil. Get a large bowlful from a garden, and the children can spread it out on a polythene sheet. They can sort out roots, stones, Worms, leaves, pieces of stick, Wireworms and other small animals and any foreign matter. They can feel the grittiness of it, and can look at it with a hand-lens. A small quantity can be shaken up in a jar of water. If it is then allowed to settle the different constituents of the soil can be seen. Leaves, bits of stick etc float on top and the other particles settle on the bottom, with the lightest on top — stones, gravel, sand, clay.

2 Children can collect soil samples from different areas, put these in bottles and label them, e.g. 'Soil from Mark's garden', 'Soil from the waste ground next to the shop.'

They can see that the soils vary, particularly if the samples are collected from fairly widespread sites. Clean mayonnaise jars are suitable containers for these samples.

3 Older children can make simple soil profiles. Using a spade, they can dig a hole, and if the sides are kept straight and firm the layers of the soil can be seen (unless the top soil is very deep!). This is made easier if the children can dig a section from a bank or mound. They will see the top vegetation, the darker top soil and the lighter sub-soil. The depth of

the top soil can be measured, and compared with the depth in other places.

4 Experiments with soil should always include some on growth. Samples of soils should be put into similar pots, and each labelled to say where the soil was found, and the name of the child who found it. Pots should be kept in identical conditions and all watered at the same time with the same amount of water. Grass seed should be sprinkled on the top of the damp soil and, after two or three weeks, the rate of growth and the condition of the plants can be compared. This work is probably better for older infants who can make charts to show growth week by week.

5 If a sample of clay soil can be found, the children can feel how cold and damp it is. They can leave it to dry naturally and can see how hard it gets, and how it cracks. They can discuss whether or not plants could grow in this, and can experiment with growing, say, Pea seeds in clay soil. They can model small bricks from it and let them dry; they probably will not realize that the clay they use for pottery is a type of soil.

WORKING AND RECORDING

The youngest children can sort out a sample of soil, and can make a display of all the things they have found in it — stones, roots, pieces of stick, leaves, Earthworms, other animals, small plants, seeds, pupae, and any other things. If the soil is left to dry they can feel what it is like after all the moisture has evaporated, and they can see if there is any change of colour.

They can collect samples from different places and see if they look any different. The samples can be labelled and displayed.

Older children can shake up samples in jars of water and compare the amount of sand and stones in each sample. They can also experiment with the growing properties of the samples (see *Planning and preparation*, 4). Charts can be kept showing progress week by week:

	Pot 1	Pot 2	Pot 3
Height of grass			
Thickness			
Colour			

The children can discuss the results, but for these to be reasonably obvious see that the samples are sufficiently varied, e.g. clay soil, very sandy soil, soil that is mostly stones etc as well as some samples of loam.

Soil profiles can be shown by using thick card strips. If these are put against the profile the layers can be marked on it, and the thickness of top soil, from different situations, can be compared. If this is not

A simplified soil profile

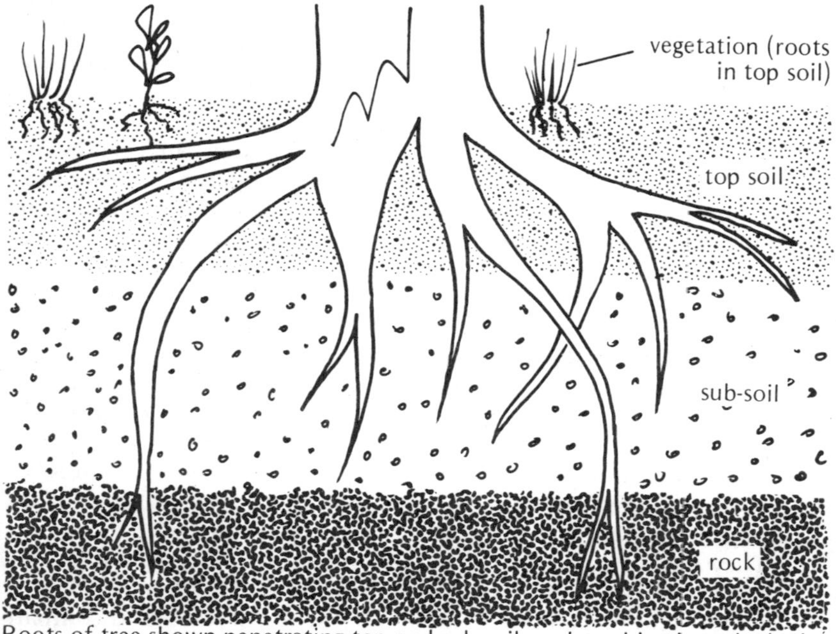

Roots of tree shown penetrating top and sub-soil, and reaching into the bed rock.

practical children can cut sections into the ground and can measure how far down the roots of grass plants, Dandelions or Groundsel grow.

Children can be asked to suggest their own experiments. For example, can they devise an experiment to find out how quickly water will drain through a given sample?

Older infants can collect and try to name any animals found in the soil. If they find pupae they can keep these and see if they hatch. The pupae will need to be kept in damp soil and in a box with a top (a piece of nylon stocking stretched over the top and secured with a rubber band). The children can label the boxes and talk about the pupae to other children.

They can write a book on 'All We Have Found Out About Soil' or they can make a soil frieze. If this is made as if they are looking at a section of the ground, they can add all the things they have found in the soil, the depths of the layers, the types of plants growing on the surface, and any other surface features such as rocks and trees. The roots of the trees can be shown going down into the deeper layers.

A soil display can be arranged. The children can put the different things they have found into boxes with brief notes explaining each exhibit, e.g.

> This exhibition tells you all the things we have found out about the soil in the park.
> These are the types of plants that grow on different soils in this area.
> These Pea plants have been grown in soils from different places. Can you tell which is the best soil?

Make sure that the children who have done the work get the credit for it and that all exhibits are labelled with the proper notes and the children's names. Even if the children are too young to write the labels or to read them, and you have to do it for them, they should decide what the wording is to be.

SUPPORT MATERIAL

Books for the children

Sciencewise Book 3 Sheila Parker and Alan Ward (Nelson)

Books for teacher reference

The Puffin Book of Gardening Mary Kelly (Penguin Books)
Early Experiences Science 5/13 (Macdonald Educational)
Looking Around in Town and Country Philip Sauvain (Franklin Watts)
Using the Environment: Investigations 2 Science 5/13 (Macdonald Educational)

Useful apparatus

Margarine pots with lids (for collecting samples); plastic bowls; polythene sheeting; trowels and spoons; small spades; mayonnaise jars; glass and plastic jars with lids; boxes for display (shoebox lids etc); strips of thick card; hand-lenses; grass and Pea seeds; flower pots or yoghurt pots.

7 LOOKING AT A TREE

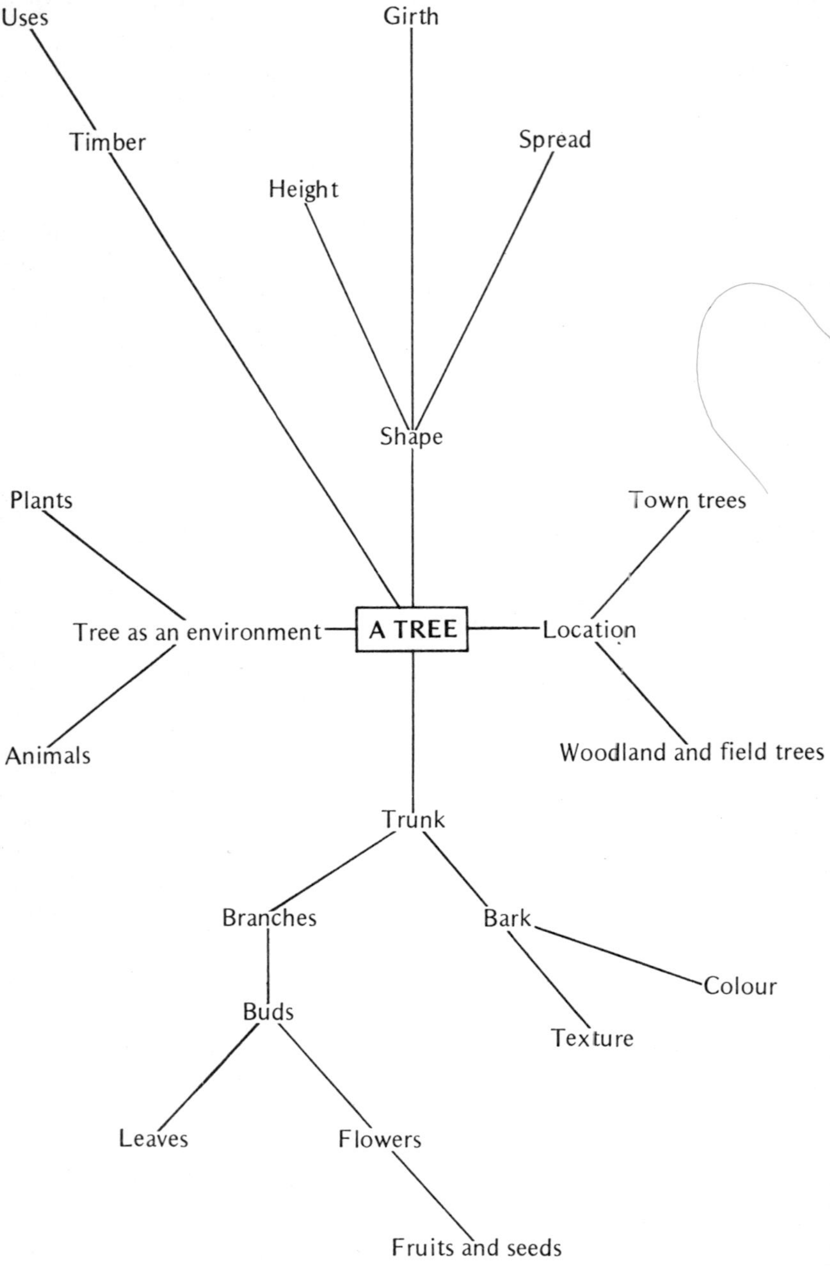

Trees can be found almost anywhere, and even a single tree can provide the basis for study, but looking at trees in general is too big a topic for small children. They will find it difficult to remember the characteristics of different species, and they need to be able to read fluently if they are to identify even the commonest trees from a book. It is, however, never too early to introduce them to trees in the hope that they will eventually realize how important it is to care for, to conserve and to plant them.

If a tree is introduced as a habitat for other living things it is likely to prove more interesting than just collecting leaves, identifying them and making collections of them as a means of classifying the trees in the area.

Any available tree can be looked at, though an old Oak or Horse Chestnut is likely to attract children from the beginning. They are massive, well-shaped trees and the children are already familiar with the acorn and the 'conker'. It is always easier to start from the familiar and then to introduce the detail. If the only possible specimen is something like a badly trimmed Plane or Lime growing alongside the pavement then this will do! There are a great many things to be learnt from trees in towns and such a study could be the prelude to a visit to a park, a woodland area or a garden.

GENERAL NOTES

1 Children recognize trees from a very early age, but they seldom realize that they are plants and have the characteristics of plants. They are woody perennials with a single stem (or trunk) which may divide close to the ground. The flowers of trees are very varied and may be spectacular like the Horse Chestnut or fairly inconspicuous like the Ash. The children may already know what the blossom of Apples, Pears and Plums looks like. In some species there are separate male flowers and female flowers, sometimes growing on different trees, e.g. Willow and Holly.

2 Trees reach a maximum height and spread and then stop growing, but the circumference of the trunk and branches increases, however slightly, during every year that the tree is alive. Children are often interested in some facts about trees, e.g.

Oak wood is very hard and strong and will last a very long time. Oak trees produce their best timber when they are over 150 years old. They do not even produce acorns until they are about sixty years old.

The Wellingtonia is the largest growing plant in the world. In its native California it can grow over 100 m tall. In the Sequoia National Park there are specimens over 100 m tall, with a girth of over 27 m and with bark more than 0.5 m thick. They can live well over 3000 years.

The word 'beam' is the Anglo-Saxon word for tree — hence Whitebeam and Hornbeam.

The Christmas tree is really a Spruce — one of the Conifers.

3 Trees can be grouped as:

a Broad leaved, e.g. Lime, Beech, Oak, Horse Chestnut, Plane. Most of them shed their leaves in the autumn. (The Holly is an exception.)

b Narrow leaved, e.g. the Conifers. Most of these are evergreens. (The Larch is an exception.)

4 In young trees the bark is usually thin and smooth, but this gets thicker and more ridged with age. The characteristics of the wood are particular to each tree and are too difficult for younger children to study, but they will know that some things are made of wood and they can look at the different examples around them, ranging from buildings and furniture to tool handles, pencils and matches.

5 Trees are not only beautiful to look at and interesting to study, but their fallen leaves provide valuable humus, their roots bind the soil together and so prevent erosion, and they provide shelter and a habitat for a wide variety of living organisms. They provide timber, but trees cut down need to be replaced by new ones if our woodlands are to survive for future generations.

6 The roots of trees spread out as far underground as the branches do overground. Some of the roots penetrate deep into the sub-soil and the basic rock. This is necessary for anchorage and to ensure that the tree reaches plentiful water supplies.

7 For identifying trees a good, basic book will be needed. I would recommend *A Field Guide to the Trees of Britain and Northern Europe* by Alan Mitchell.

PLANNING AND PREPARATION

1 If children are to study a particular tree choose, if possible, a fully-grown Oak, Horse Chestnut, Beech, Plane or Sycamore growing in a field or park (or where there is growth underneath it). If there is no choice then make the best possible use of what is available. Make sure that you can identify the tree; the children are sure to ask you what it is! Visit it yourself and note any particular features that would merit discussion. Does the tree appear to be fully grown? Is it an old or young tree? At the time you are looking, are there any flowers or fruits to be seen? Are there any algae or fungi growing on it? Are there any signs of animal life (caterpillars, Oak Galls, Spiders' webs etc)?

2 First let the children look at the tree as a whole — its shape, circumference of the trunk (can two children join hands round the trunk?), its height and the spread of the branches. They can measure the circumference of the trunk with string. Officially this is measured 1.5 m from the ground but let the children measure at a height they can reach. With older children overall height can be estimated, using a child for

comparison. They can also gauge the distance between the ground and the first branch.

3 Get children to look at:

Bark — thickness, texture, colour, pattern of ridges. If any bark has fallen off they can look at this, but stress the fact that bark must not be torn off a tree.

Leaves — shape, size, colour, whether single or compound (a leaf made up of several leaflets such as Horse Chestnut or Ash), pattern of veins.

Buds — shape, size, position on twigs, significant features (such as the sticky buds of Horse Chestnut).

Flowers, fruits and seeds (according to the season) — size, shape, colour, special features (wings of Sycamore seeds, cones etc). Some seeds can be collected for growing in pots in the classroom.

Leaf fall — time when the leaves start to fall, change of colour, leaf scars on the twigs.

4 Notice if there are any other plants associated with the tree:

a Plants growing on the tree such as the green alga seen on the trunk. This will indicate the direction of the prevailing rainfall, as the alga grows on the wettest side of the trunk. There may be fungi growing from the trunk or branches. Some grow on living trees and some only grow on dead and decaying trees. Mistletoe may be seen on some trees. The seed is carried by a bird and rubbed off onto the trunk, and if it gets into a crack it may germinate. Mistletoe will only grow on a living tree as it needs to take food from the growing tissues.

b Plants growing under the tree. Vegetation will vary according to habitat. For example, very little grows under Pine trees. The thick layer of needles decays slowly, but Foxgloves and Bracken may be found. Children can look for Ferns, Grasses, small flowering plants, Heathers and Mosses. They can see if the vegetation differs near the trunk and on the edge of the branch spread, and can talk about the effects of light and rain on growing plants. There may be fungi growing near the base of the tree and children can look at these. (*Note* Some of these may be poisonous, so if you are not sure do not let the children handle them.)

5 See if there are any animals associated with the tree:

a Bird visitors. Do birds visit the tree? (It will not matter if the children cannot name them). Are there any signs of nests? If the tree is in woodland the children may find Owl pellets under the tree. These are pellets of indigestible material regurgitated by Owls, and they indicate what the birds have been feeding on. Small bones, fur and insect wing cases can be found in these pellets.

b Caterpillars. These may be found on the leaves either singly or in groups. Some of these can be kept in the classroom and fed on the leaves off the tree. It is also possible to enclose them in a bag on the tree. Make a bag from nylon mesh or from a piece of a nylon stocking. Enclose the end of the branch in this and tie the open ends

A 'caterpillar' bag

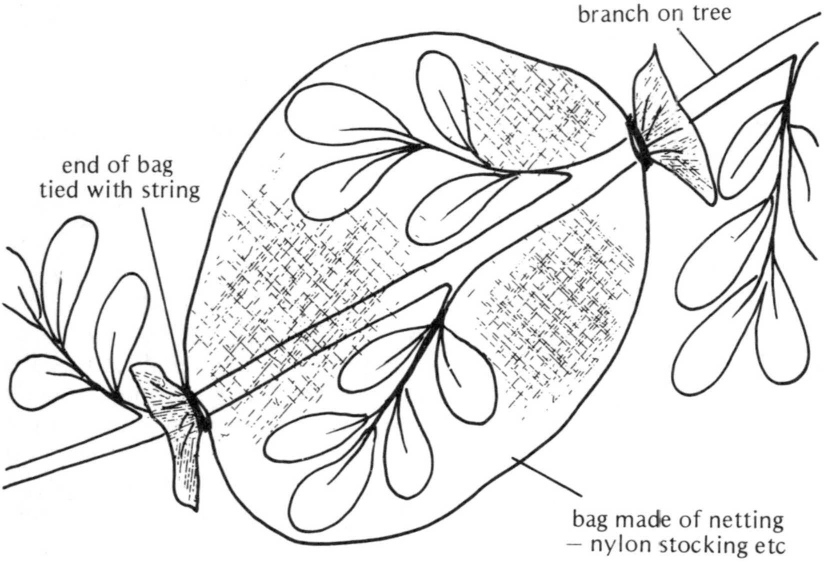

with string. In this way the caterpillars can be kept on their food plant but can be watched. Many of these caterpillars pupate underground so they will either have to be released or put in a jar with soil when they are fully grown.

c If there is any loose bark look underneath for signs of Bark Beetles. They make branched tunnels as they chew through the bark, and some of the beetles may be found.

d Spiders can often be found in cracks in the bark, and the children may see the round cocoons attached under loose bark.

e Let the children look in the litter (fallen leaves and other debris) under the tree, if it is in a suitable location, and see if they can find other small animals — Earwigs, Woodlice, Centipedes.

f See if there are any other signs of larger animals, such as Rabbit droppings or torn bark where a Cat constantly scratches.

WORKING AND RECORDING

Once the children are interested, a tree will become very important to them, and even with the very youngest it is possible to sustain interest over several weeks. They can look at the tree they are studying, paying special attention to the leaves and the bark. They can make rubbings of both of these. They will need only large wax crayons and strong, thin paper. One child can hold the paper while the other scribbles over it. With the youngest infants the results may not be very good at first but children enjoy doing this and their efforts can be trimmed and mounted for display.

A large paper silhouette, showing the correct shape of the tree, can be made, and the children can then make pictures to stick on this showing what they have found. For example, the outline of an Oak tree might have pictures to show, say, three birds, a Spider on the trunk, several caterpillars, acorns on the tree and on the ground, some Oak Galls on the tree, and two Toadstools, some grass, two Earwigs and several Woodlice under the tree.

Older infants can make a tree profile showing the features of the tree in the spring, summer and winter. They can make rubbings of the leaves at different stages, draw pictures of the flowers and fruit, and collect such things as Oak Galls, feathers, pieces of broken bark etc. Leaves can be pressed by putting them between several layers of newspaper and then putting them under a heavy weight (such as a cupboard) for several weeks.

They can also make plaster casts of leaves and buds. To make plaster casts get a thick, flat block of Plasticine, press the twig or leaf into this to make a clear impression, make a wall round the block with thin card or a strip of Plasticine and pour in plaster of paris. After this has set the Plasticine can be peeled off and the cast painted and varnished.

Put a large sheet of white paper or a piece of sheeting under the tree and shake a branch. Any small animals falling off the tree can be seen easily on the sheet. Children can also find the area of branch spread by marking its outline, on the ground, with string. This will also indicate where the lateral roots reach, and where there will be the maximum amount of drip from the ends of branches.

Having looked at the tree, books can be used to find out more about this particular type of tree, and a tree exhibition can be mounted.

An Oak Tree Exhibition, for example, could include a tree silhouette with pictures of plants and animals found on it, leaf and bark rubbings, plaster casts, pressed leaves, examples of acorns and bark, a small twig to show buds and some written work about the differences in the tree in winter and summer. The children can also find out the uses of Oak timber — Elizabethan ships, timbered houses, furniture, etc. and can include pictures of these. They can take photographs and show their tree from several angles and, if possible, during several seasons. They can include interesting historical notes such as the importance of acorns in the past for feeding pigs in the winter, and the fact that the children of the villages were sent out to collect these. Acorns can be shown growing in pots and if children know where any Oak trees can be found they could include a simple map to show where they are, or they can say where they know Oak trees to be growing.

If they are making an exhibition of a tree in a town park or along a road they can include other relevant details. For example, a tree growing in the pavement may have been trimmed (often very badly) and show signs of abnormal or stunted growth, and the trunk may have been damaged by having notices nailed onto it or being hit by cars. The leaves may show a thick layer of dirt which makes them look drab and unhealthy. However, the tree is growing, and it would be interesting to see how well it survives air pollution. How many cars, on average, go down the road every day? Also, if the tree is paved or concreted all round how is it managing to grow? Are the roots pushing up the ground anywhere? The older children could try and find out if the local authority or the Department of Town and Country Planning have any plans for planting more trees, or replacing ones that are dying.

Once children have been given the opportunity to really look at one tree they may want to look at other trees. Find out if there are any nature trails near you, if there are any parks with several examples of trees, if there is an area of woodland or forest which you could visit or if there are fields with hedges where you could take children. Teach them straightaway that they must not rip off branches or bark, and that a tree must not be damaged in any way.

SUPPORT MATERIAL

Books for the children

The Tree and its World Romola Showell (Ladybird Books)
Look at Trees Starters Series (Macdonald Educational)
Trees Edited by Jean Imrie (A. & C. Black)
Plants B.J. Bampton (Macmillan)

Books for teacher reference

A Field Guide to the Trees of Britain and Northern Europe Alan Mitchell (Collins)
Trees Science 5/13 (Macdonald Educational)
The Ecology of Woodlands Alfred Leutscher (Franklin Watts)
The Observer's Book of Trees Herbert Edlin (Warne)

Useful apparatus

Flower pots; Plasticine; plaster of paris; wax crayons; hand-lenses; small jars with nylon-mesh tops; nylon-mesh bags; string; camera; boxes for mounting specimens (see Section 22 *Collecting Things*); piece of sheeting.

8 INSECTS

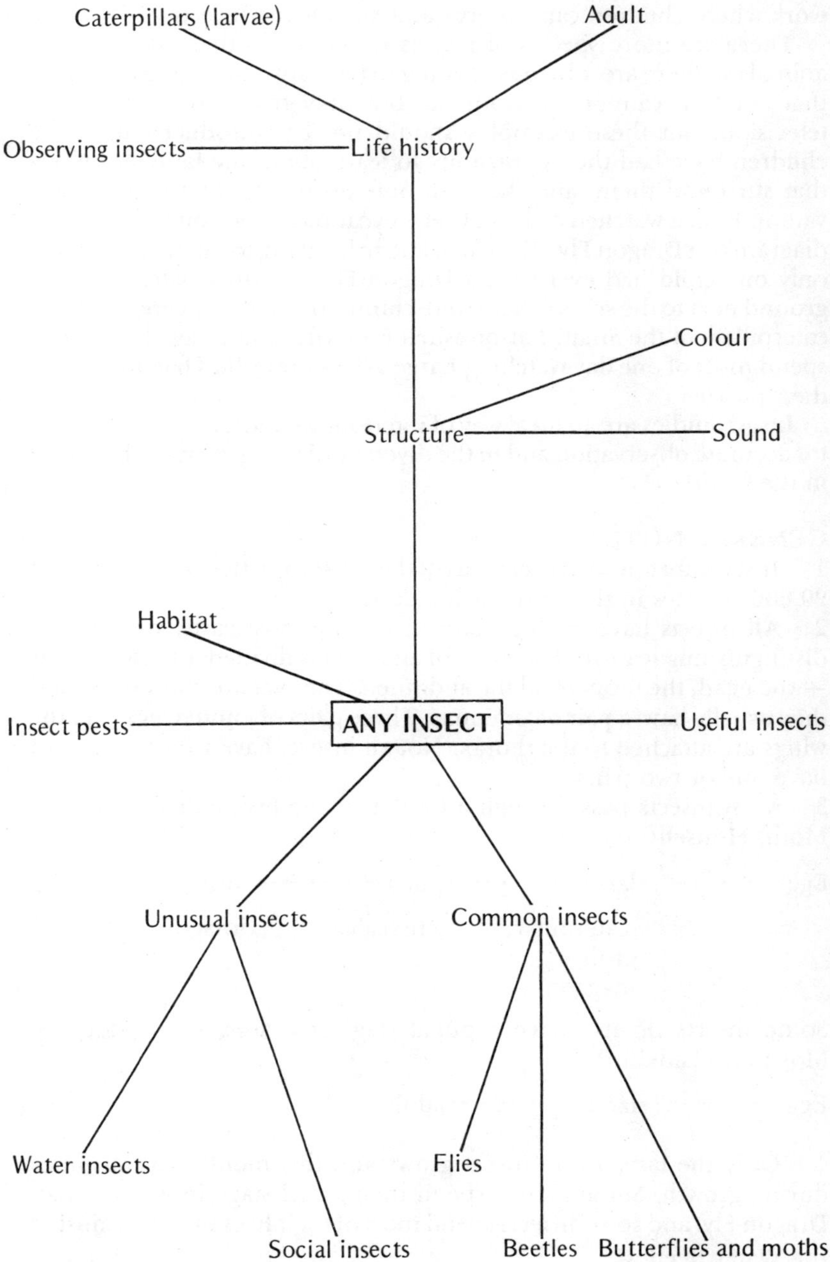
Caterpillars (larvae)
Adult
Observing insects
Life history
Colour
Structure
Sound
Habitat
Insect pests
ANY INSECT
Useful insects
Unusual insects
Common insects
Water insects
Flies
Social insects
Beetles
Butterflies and moths

With so many insects about it is not difficult to choose specimens that children can actually see. When, for example, Ladybirds, Houseflies, Ants and Wasps can be collected so easily it is a simple matter to plan work where children can observe and keep living insects.

There are more species of insects in the world than of any other animals so there are, obviously, going to be many interesting examples that children cannot see from life but only from books, film and television, but these examples should not be introduced until the children have had the opportunity to learn about the familiar insects that surround them, and they can only do this by first-hand observation. I once watched a class of seven year olds laboriously copying a diagram of a Dragon Fly off the blackboard; talking to them I found that only one child had ever seen a Dragon Fly, but on a patch of waste ground next to the school there were clumps of Nettles covered with the caterpillars of the Small Tortoiseshell Butterfly; and I have had a class spend most of one day watching Large White Butterflies hatching from their pupae.

Insect studies are an ideal way of interesting children in the necessity for accurate observation and in the diversity of living things to be found in the world.

GENERAL NOTES

1 Insects are found in every part of the world, and there are more than 20,000 species in the British Isles alone.

2 All insects have six legs, and this is the most easily recognized, distinguishing feature. The body of an insect is divided into three parts — the head, the thorax and the abdomen. The eyes are compound and they usually have a pair of antennae. Three pairs of jointed legs, and the wings are attached to the thorax. Not all insects have wings, but most have one or two pairs.

3 Most insects pass through a four-stage life history, e.g. Butterfly, Moth, Housefly.

Egg →→→→→	larva →→→→→	pupa →→→→→	adult
	(caterpillar, grub, maggot)	(chrysalis)	(imago)

Some insects do not have a pupal stage, e.g. Stick Insect, Earwig, Mosquito, Ladybird.

Egg →→→→→ larva →→→→→ adult

4 Only the larva of an insect grows and this moults several times during growth. Some insects spend their larval stage in water (Gnat, Dragon Fly) and some insects spend most of their lives in water (most of the Water Beetles).

5 Classification of insects is far too complicated a subject for young children, but they will more readily understand the enormous number of insects if they learn some of the major groups. These could be very simply classified as:

Butterflies and Moths
Flies
Beetles
Ants, Wasps and Bees
Crickets and Grasshoppers

PLANNING AND PREPARATION

1 Insects can be kept quite easily and it is worthwhile taking the trouble to do this so that the children can watch them develop. The easiest to keep are the caterpillars of Butterflies and Moths. See that the children understand that caterpillars will only feed on their own particular food plants, so that if they find a caterpillar they must bring a leaf of the plant on which they found it, so that it can be fed.

If caterpillars are to be kept they need to be housed properly, and kept in conditions in which they will survive. Large plastic sweet jars are easily obtainable and can be used very successfully. A piece of nylon

A caterpillar cage

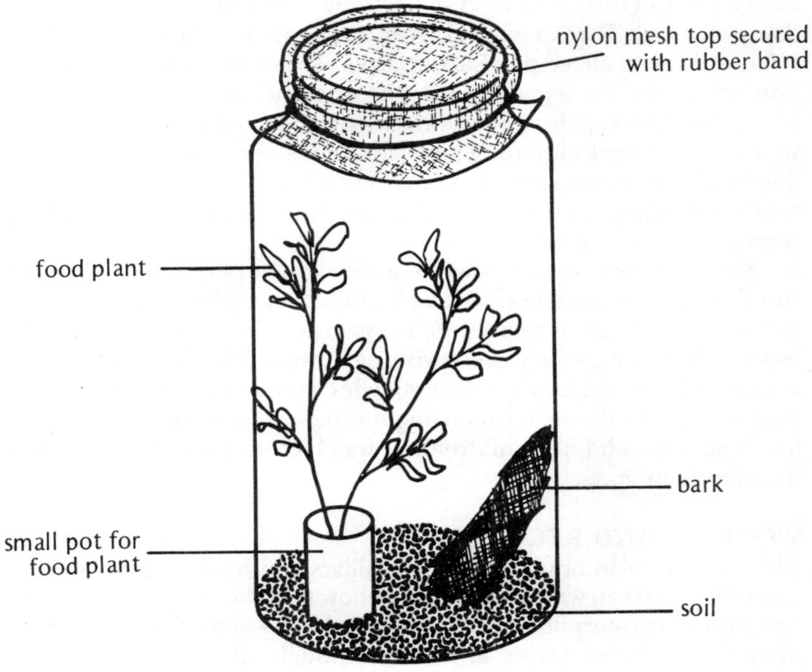

mesh (from tights), can be secured with a rubber band, and can be used as a cover. To keep the food plant fresh put the stems in a small jar of water; put a strip of cotton wool round the top of the jar to prevent small caterpillars from falling into the water. Collapsible cages can be made using two equal-sized tin lids, and a piece of rolled acetate sheet. Roll the acetate sheet so that it will fit into one of the lids, and stick down the edge with adhesive tape. Perforate the other lid and use it for the top. The advantage of this cage is that it can be dismantled for storage. A thick layer of damp soil should be put in the bottom of each cage for those caterpillars which pupate underground, and a small piece of bark or wood for those which normally cling to a fence or tree trunk.

2 The common Stick Insects kept in many schools are natives of India. They are stick-like wingless insects with six long legs. They feed on privet and will moult several times before they are fully grown. The insects (which are bisexual) will each lay up to 500 eggs during a lifetime. The eggs laid in the autumn will hatch the following spring, and the insects live for several months. While these can be kept in a large jar, like the caterpillars, the children can be helped to make cages for them out of shoe boxes. Cut a large rectangle from a shoe-box lid and tape cellophane over this to make an observation window. Air holes can be punched in the sides of the box, and the food plant can be kept fresh by putting it in a small jar of water.

3 Earwigs can be kept in a large jar, or box with a mesh cover. They need a piece of turf and a layer of decaying leaves which should be kept damp (not wet). The Earwigs will live quite happily in this for some time. It is not always realized that Earwigs have wings and can fly, and they are unusual in that the female guards the eggs and newly-hatched larvae.

4 Ants can be kept for a short time in a flat box — a plastic seed tray — with a piece of dark glass or perspex for a lid. The tray should be loosely filled with soil, leaving a gap at one corner where the ants can be fed with small quantities of jam or honey. They also need some protein, and will soon pick clean a small bone.

5 Outdoor excursions to look for insects can be planned. Look under stones and fallen branches, but teach children to replace them. They are the natural habitat of many small organisms. Look on the bark and leaves of trees, and watch insects visiting flowers. The children can go to a pond or stream to look for Water Beetles, and they can always look for Wasps, Flies etc. If insects which might sting — such as Wasps — are put into a jar with a lid, the children can watch them for a short time and then let them go.

WORKING AND RECORDING

Children can plan how to keep caterpillars and how to care for them. The older ones can write an account of how they did this, and develop it into a book on caterpillar care. If they watch the whole life cycle they can draw the different stages and make models of these out of clay, Plasticine, felt etc.

On a warm sunny day the children can put out brightly coloured pieces of paper and material (red, blue, green, yellow, orange, pink etc) and see which colour insects seem to prefer. They can make a chart of the results.

The younger infants can make an insect frieze with pictures (drawn by themselves) of all the insects they have seen, and these can be named.

Using the pictures, models, live exhibits, poems etc an insect exhibition can be put together. Taped commentaries can be made for the other children visiting the exhibition.

Older infants can make insect inventories and insect counts, e.g.

Name	No wings	1 pair of wings	2 pairs of wings
Housefly			

Where insects were seen

Name	Indoors	On the ground	On plants	Flying	Near water
Ladybird					

An insect count					Date Place				
Butter-fly	**Fly**	**Lady-bird**	**Ant**	**Gnat**	**Bee**	**Wasp**	**Lace-wing**		

Following work from actual observation, some topics about other insects could be planned. Film, film-strips, slides, pictures and reference books can be used to show the children what these look like. For example:

Insect Pests — Mosquitos, Locusts, Houseflies, caterpillar pests etc
Useful Insects — Honey Bees, Silk Moths, Ladybirds etc
Unusual Insects — Froghoppers (larvae make 'cuckoo spit'), Water Boatmen, Fleas (who can jump many times their own height) etc
Beetles
Insects that Sting
Butterflies and Moths
The Honey Bee

The Honey Bee particularly appeals to young children, and they can see its life history on film-strip (Ladybird produce a film-strip to go with their book *The Life of the Honey Bee*). They can make a 'Honey Bee Book' and have a honey-eating session!

SUPPORT MATERIAL

Books for the children

Insects You Can Find Starters Series (Macdonald Educational)
Insects Little Learning Library Series (Basil Blackwell)
Let's Look at Insects Deborah Manley (Ward Lock)
Butterflies, Moths and other Insects S.A. Manning (Ladybird Books)
Insects Mollie Clarke (Hart-Davis)
Caterpillars Mollie Clarke (Hart-Davis)
Bees Starters Series (Macdonald Educational)

Books for teacher reference

The Oxford Book of Insects John Burton (OUP)

Useful apparatus

Sweet jars; nylon mesh; rubber bands; hand-lenses; shoe boxes; jars of different sizes; felt; modelling clay; acetate sheet; tin lids.

9 KEEPING SNAILS, SPIDERS AND OTHER SMALL ANIMALS

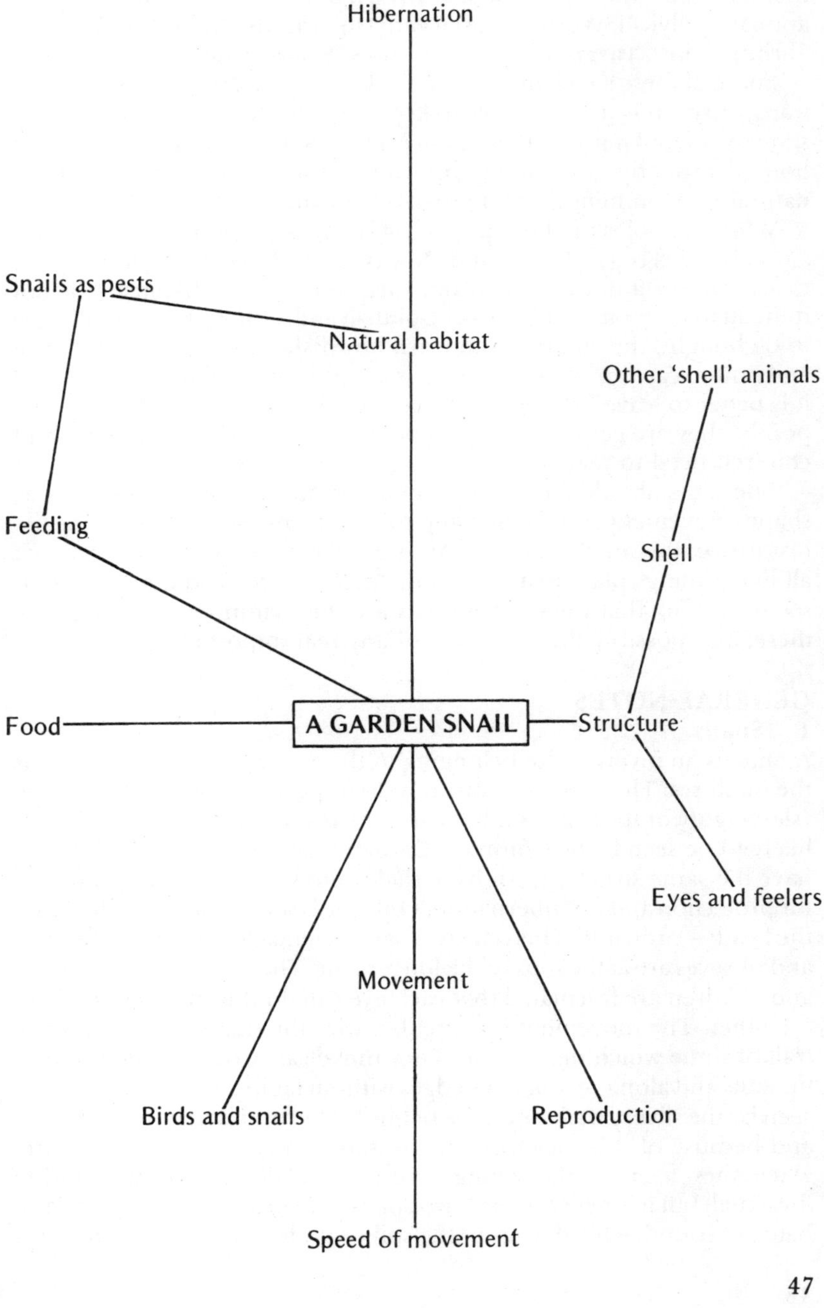

The group of living things called animals can be divided into two groups — the vertebrates (which have an internal skeleton of bones) and the invertebrates. The vertebrates are the mammals, the birds, the reptiles, the fish and the amphibians. Invertebrates include single-celled animals, Jellyfish, Worms, crustaceans (such as the Crabs, Lobsters and Shrimps), insects, Spiders and molluscs (Snails, Slugs, 'shellfish' etc).

Some of these small animals can be kept by children so that they can watch them. It is not advisable to keep them for long periods (children soon tire of looking after them), but even for a short time they need to be housed properly, and so children need to know something of their natural environment if the animals are to survive.

Whilst tadpoles can be kept easily it is not as simple to keep the adult animals, so Frogs, Toads and Newts should be brought into the classroom for a day and then returned to their own habitat. It is not difficult to keep one or two small Goldfish and, although these will have to be bought, the children can learn how fishes move, their structure and how to care for them. Unless it is possible to provide a natural pool it is better to leave fish such as Minnows and Sticklebacks in their own ponds; they are getting scarcer as pools and streams are filled in, and children need to realize the value of preserving wild life.

The aims should be to teach children to observe such things as shape, movement and feeding and to understand something of the life histories of the smaller animals. We should try to establish the idea that all living things play their part in the cycle of life. Too often children seem to think that the only animals are the mammals, and that only these, and possibly the birds, are of any real importance.

GENERAL NOTES

1 Snails

A Snail is an invertebrate belonging to the group of animals known as the molluscs. There are over one hundred species of Snail in the British Isles; eighty of these live on land and the rest in water. The Snail most likely to be seen is the Common Garden Snail, but basically all Snails have the same structure. All have shells into which they can withdraw for protection and for hibernation. Only the bottom part — the foot and the head — protrude. There are two pairs of tentacles in the Land Snails, and the eyes are at the tops of the longer pair. The eyes can be retracted, and children are fascinated that each eye can do this independently of the other. The movement is muscular, with the snails moving along a trail of slime which they exude. They move easily over rough ground, up walls and along very narrow edges without falling. Their paths can be seen by the silvery trail they leave behind. The food is mainly vegetable, and because of this they can be a nuisance to gardeners, particularly when they feed off the young seedlings. Snails are hermaphrodite (bisexual) but it is necessary for two snails to mate before they both lay a batch of round, whitish eggs in the soil or under stones. Garden Snails are mature in about two years, and it is possible for them to live for several years. When taking children out it is possible to find a pile of broken snail shells, usually near a large stone. This is where a Thrush has been breaking the shells to eat the soft body inside. Pond Snails spend their lives in water. The eggs are laid on the underside of water plants, and look like a blob of jelly with brown dots in it. When the Snails hatch they are tiny miniatures of the adults. These Snails do not have eyes at the tips of the tentacles, but at the base of the longer pair.

2 **Spiders**

Children tend to find it difficult to distinguish between insects and Spiders, but if the legs are counted there is an obvious difference — insects have six legs and Spiders have eight. Insects have bodies divided into three parts but a Spider's is only divided into two — a large abdomen and a head. There are estimated to be over 30,000 species of Spiders in the world; six hundred of these are found in Britain and all these are harmless to humans. Not all Spiders make webs, but all can make silk. The silk is used for cocooning eggs and prey. Those that make webs make them to trap food; they build them in a place where they are most likely to catch flies and other insects. Spiders use their poison fangs to kill, or stun, their prey. Incredibly fine, strong silk is produced from spinnerets at the end of the abdomen. When a Spider climbs its web it loops it up behind its back legs, and then discards the length of web at the end of the climb.

3 **Woodlice**

Woodlice spend most of their time in the dark, and can be found under stones, fallen wood and in the litter under hedges and in woods. One type of Woodlouse – the Pill Woodlouse – rolls into a ball when frightened. The Woodlouse is the only land-living relative of the Crabs and Shrimps, and is about 12 mm long when fully grown. It feeds mainly on rotting vegetable matter, and passes through several moults while growing. Several broods of eggs are produced, the female carrying these in a pouch under her body. The eggs hatch out inside the pouch in a few weeks, and the young Woodlice emerge.

4 **Centipedes**

Centipedes are found when stones or logs are moved, and although the name means 'a hundred legs' these vary from seventeen to over a hundred pairs. They are carnivorous animals and kill their prey – mostly small Worms, insects and Spiders — by injecting poison. Eggs are laid in damp soil in the spring and summer, and once hatched the Centipede takes about three years to fully mature. Centipedes move their numerous legs in rhythmical waves as they move.

5 **Shore life**

Shore animals are not easy to keep, and it is better to let the children see specimens in their natural habitat wherever this is possible. Sea Anemones are strange animals seen on rocks as the tide recedes. They have a domed-shaped formation of tentacles. These can be withdrawn and are used for trapping prey. Barnacles and Limpets are found clinging to rocks, and the 'shells' which are likely to be seen include the Hermit Crab (this is not really a shell fish, but a type of Crab which inhabits a Periwinkle or Whelk shell), Mussels, Periwinkles, Whelks and Top Shells.

There are many other small animals to be seen, but there are several good, specialized books to help the teacher contemplating a shore study.

PLANNING AND PREPARATION

1 Keeping Spiders

The best Spiders for children to keep for observation are the Common House Spiders, or the Garden Spider. Any large jar will do for a cage, but if these animals are going to be kept frequently it is probably better to make something special. A square biscuit tin can have the sides heightened with four sheets of perspex, taped together at the corners. The original lid can then be used on top of these. If the lid is lifted frequently any webs are going to be destroyed so it is better to make a hole (the size of a cork) in the lid through which the Spiders can be given food and water. The hole can be sealed with cotton wool. Put several branches in the box, and a twig with some leaves on it, but leave the

A spider or caterpillar cage

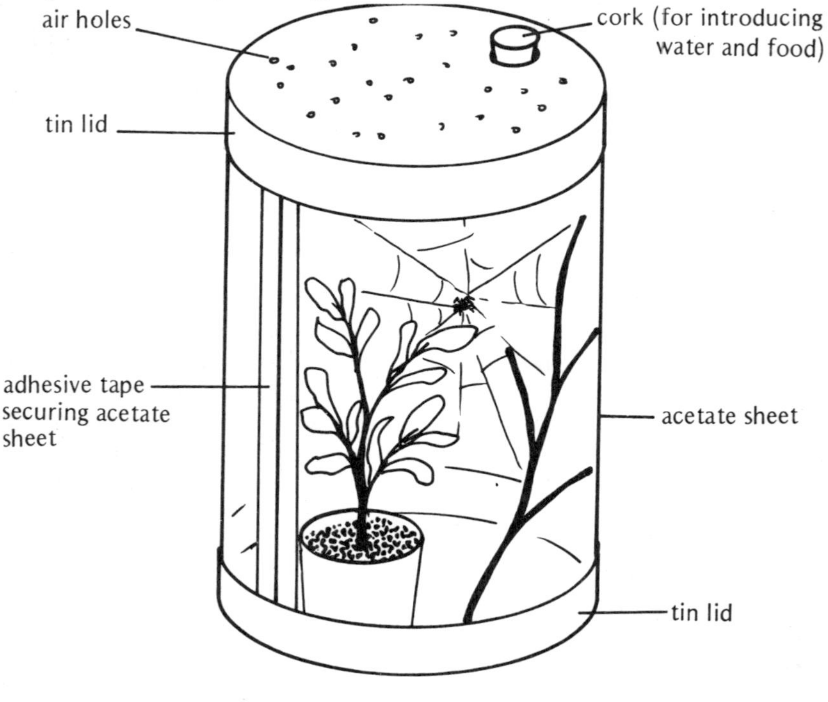

Spiders room for spinning. Alternatively, two equal-sized tin lids and a piece of rolled acetate sheet can be used, as described on page 44. Spiders like water so a few drops need to be put in through the hole daily, and small live Flies can be introduced the same way.

With very small children it is probably better to tape the lid in place or the Spiders will be let out. A Garden Spider, in a big enough cage, will make its typical wheel-shaped web, and will catch any flies in it. Children can keep Spiders for a short time in any jar, where they can watch them and feed them.

2 Keeping Snails

Snails can be kept in any large, strong box with a glass or fine-mesh lid. If glass is used the edges can be taped with masking tape, and the whole sheet covered with transparent plastic adhesive sheet, so that even if it is dropped the glass will crack and break but will not splinter. If glass is not considered safe, transparent plastic can be tacked to a wooden frame and used as a lid. The box will need a good layer of damp soil at the bottom, and several stones. Pile these up so that the Snails can get inbetween them. Give Snails fresh green food every day, but remove any that is not eaten by the following morning. Keep the box in a cool shady place. If the children want to see how a Snail moves, put it on a piece of glass and look from underneath. The regular muscular movements of the foot are easy to see. If the Snail refuses to come out of the shell dip it quickly in warm water.

3 Keeping Water Snails

Pond Snails are very easy to keep, and children like preparing a tank for them. Any fish tank will do, but a large plastic washing up bowl will be quite suitable if there is nothing else. Put a layer of sand and clean stones on the bottom, and anchor water weeds with stones or plant them in small pots (with a layer of small stones on the surface of the soil). Water weed is essential. It is the main food of the Snails, and they will eat a considerable quantity. If the tank is big enough one or two small Goldfish could be kept in the same tank, but these will need to be fed with proprietary fish food. The Snails will help keep the tank or bowl clean by feeding on the green alga which tends to grow on the sides.

4 Keeping Woodlice and Centipedes

Do not keep these animals together but they can be kept in similar boxes. Rectangular or square plastic boxes with holes punched in the lids will make suitable homes for them. Damp, rotting leaves and stones can be put into the box and the Woodlice will live quite happily for some time. Centipedes will soon kill any other small insects etc found in the rotting leaves and can then be given Greenfly to feed on. They cannot be kept for very long successfully.

WORKING AND RECORDING

The important part of the work when keeping small animals is preparing homes for them, caring for them and observing them. This is probably sufficient for the youngest infants, particularly if they are given the opportunity to talk about their animals. They can collect pictures of Snails, Spiders etc and can display these as a background for their living specimens. Older children can tell another class how, say, the spider house was prepared and how the Spiders are cared for. This could be taped for future use. Books can be made for each particular specimen, e.g. 'All about Snails', 'Spiders', 'Keeping Water Snails' etc.

If the children have already done some work on insects they can go outside and see how many small animals they can find, and a list (illustrated) could be made for the school, e.g.

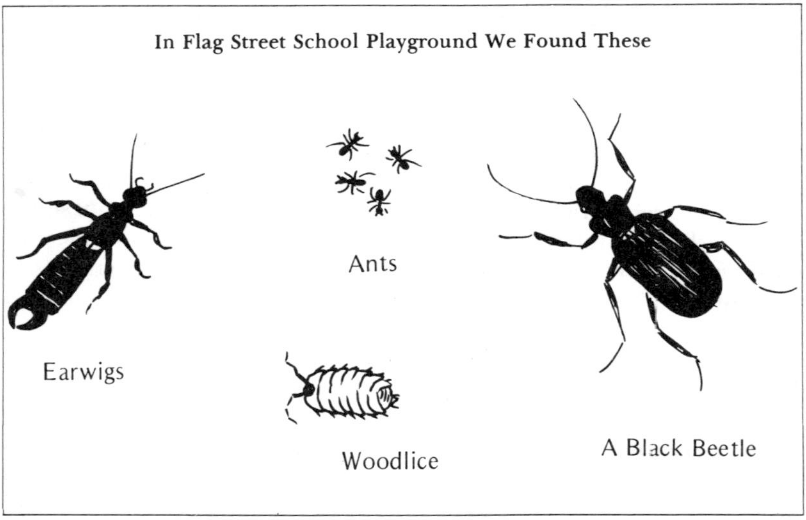

They can make inventories based on the number of legs:

Name	No. legs	6 legs	8 legs	More than 8 legs

Older infants can make a card index system for all the animals they are likely to see. Each card can consist of the name (written in large letters at the top) and basic characteristics. These can be discussed with the children, and a list made so that they will know what to include on the cards. It is better to have separate index systems for the vertebrates and the invertebrates (it can be very muddling for a young child to sort out too many characteristics), e.g.

Ladybird

This is a beetle.
Number of legs – 6.
Wing cases – Yes. Red with 7 spots.
Wings – Yes.
Where found – on dandelion.
Size – 8mm.
Food –

Side 1

Side 2

These can be put, alphabetically, into a box for adding to and future use.

Most of these animals can be a stimulus for good model work using modelling clay, felt etc. Large, flat, cut-out card pictures can be made with details added in more card or other materials, e.g. Snail head and foot; shell stuck on separately; small beads stuck on for eyes. These can be large enough for several children to work on one model.

The books about these animals can be made in the same shape as the animal, e.g. the cover of a book about Ladybirds can be the shape of the animal, and coloured red with black spots. This can be a small individual book or a large one with pages on which children's drawings and pictures can be stuck.

SUPPORT MATERIAL

Books for the children

Learning about Insects and Small Animals Romola Showell (Ladybird Books)
Very Small Animals Starters Series (Macdonald Educational)
Spiders First Library Series (Macdonald Educational)
Look Under Stones Albert James (Macdonald Educational)
All about Snails, Ladybirds and Things Althea (Holmes McDougall)

Books for teacher reference

The Oxford Book of Invertebrates D. Nichols and J.A.L. Cooke (OUP)
The Ecology of Woodlands Alfred Leutscher (Franklin Watts)

Minibeasts Science 5/13 (Macdonald Educational)
The Sea Shore John Barrett and C.M. Yonge (Collins)

Useful apparatus

Assortment of boxes and jars; nylon mesh; rubber bands; hand-lenses; large sheets of card; small fish tanks; shoe boxes; biscuit tins; transparent plastic sheet; sheets of glass, perspex or acetate.

10 ANY SMALL MAMMAL

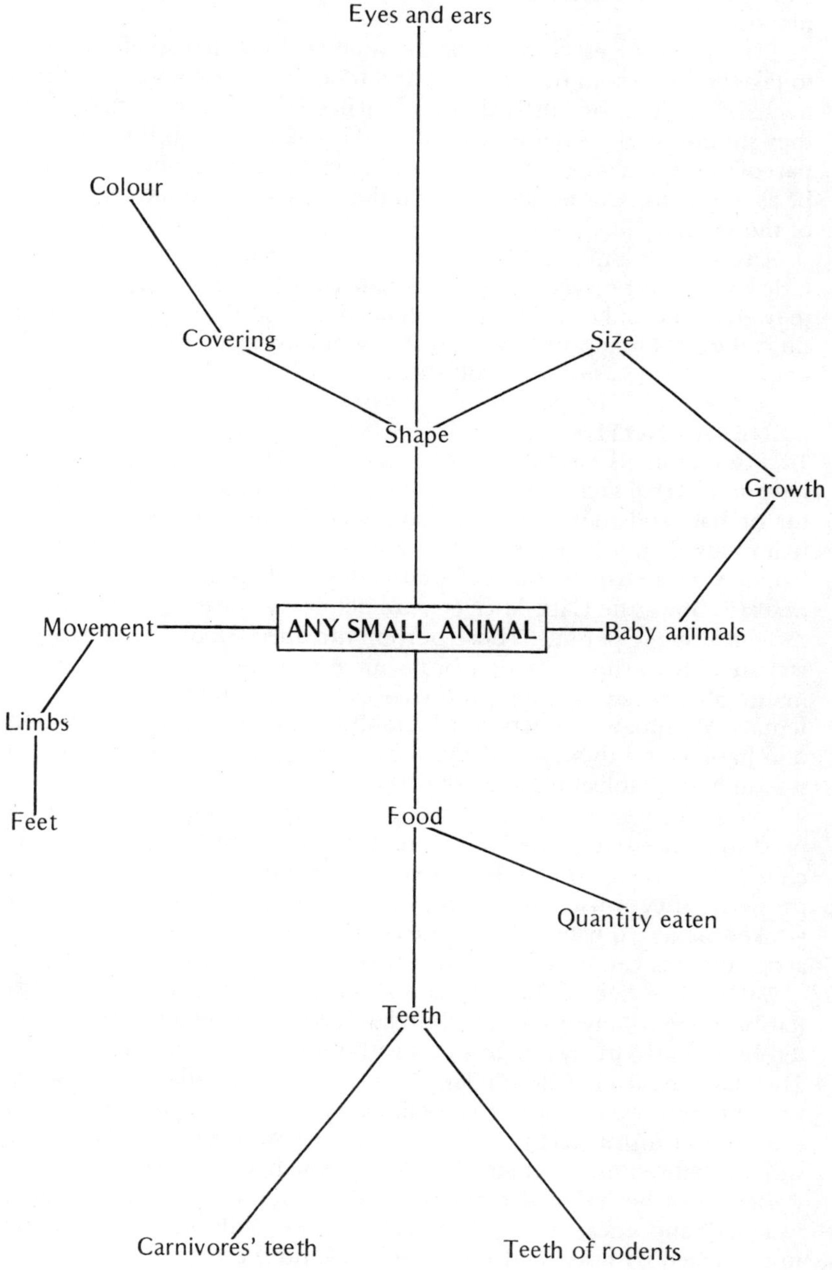

Many children are used to having pets at home or at school, but a pet should mean more than an animal in which they are interested for a short time and which, after a while, becomes a chore instead of a pleasure.

Even the youngest children can be taught to look after small animals, to take an interest in their welfare and to learn something about their lives and habits. Obviously, children will need to be helped with this but they should be given definite, even if minimal, responsibility for some part of the animal's care. Supervision is always essential, but this should be as unobtrusive as possible, so that the child feels that he is in charge of the animal.

Any work with mammals should be aimed at the basic care of pets. A little kitten may be a very attractive, small, cuddly animal, but a Cat lives to twelve years old or more, and will need to be looked after for all that time; the Rabbit may be fun to feed in the summer, but the cage has still got to be cleaned out on a cold January day!

GENERAL NOTES

1 All mammals have features in common. They are warm blooded, have an internal skeleton and four limbs, are more or less covered with fur or hair and many of them have tails. With very few exceptions mammals do not lay eggs. The young develop inside the body of the female and are usually born in a fairly developed state. Those born in nests (Rabbits, the Cats, Mice etc) are helpless at birth and need to be cared for by the parents. Those born in the open (Deer, Cows, Horses etc) are able to run soon after birth but are still fed by the female. All mammals are fed on milk produced by the mammary glands of the female. Mammals vary very considerably in size, shape, colour, feeding and habitat and there are so many interesting species that it is always possible to establish topic work with children.

2 Pets which can be kept in school are fairly limited. They usually need to be housed in reasonably small cages and to be easy to feed. If children are going to handle them (and they must be taught to do this properly) they must not bite or scratch. Animals have to be fed at weekends and during school holidays, so make sure that suitable arrangements can be made before acquiring an animal.

Rabbits The size of Rabbits varies, but the black and white Dutch Rabbits tend to stay small. The hutch must be sufficiently large for the Rabbit to move freely and to sit up without the ears touching the roof. They tame easily and do not smell if cleaned out regularly. If a pair is kept the female will produce a new litter every few weeks, and the babies must not be disturbed until they are two or three weeks old (the female will probably destroy them if they are touched when newly born). Rabbits can be handled carefully, and do not seem to mind being weighed and measured. Once used to the children they will be undisturbed by noise and movement around them.

Guinea Pigs Guinea Pigs make ideal pets. They are small, easily handled, easy to feed and do not breed too quickly. The gestation period is about ten weeks, and the young can be touched and looked at when only a few hours old. They are miniatures of the adults when born, and are covered with fur and have their eyes open. They will nibble green food and run about when less than a day old. They are nervous little animals and rarely become as tame as rabbits, but children find them very attractive.

Mice Mice can be kept indoors in small cages but they do tend to smell however clean they are kept. They can be weighed, measured and handled and are very cheap to feed. Two females will live together quite happily, but two males tend to fight.

Hamsters Hamsters are pretty little animals, fascinating to watch as they pouch their food and sit up on their hind legs, but they are basically nocturnal and are not very active by day. They will often bite if handled, but they are easy to keep and if the children are not allowed to pick them up they make good classroom pets. They need a strong case as they will chew through thin wood very quickly.

Gerbils Gerbils are very active and this makes them particularly attractive. Like hamsters they will soon chew through a wooden cage, and will often bite if handled, but they do not smell, are easy to feed and rarely keep still for long. They will chew up everything chewable and will make untidy nests from paper, material etc.

Cats I have seen a Cat kept in an infant school where the caretaker was willing to feed it and look after it out of school hours. This was a very popular pet as it wandered from class to class, sitting on the children's tables and playing with the children's small toys. He soon got used to being weighed, measured and having paint on his feet to make paw prints. He undoubtedly taught the children a great deal about animal care.

The R.S.P.C.A. produce some very good pamphlets on pet care.

PLANNING AND PREPARATION

1 All the animals mentioned — except the Cat — need special cages, and these should be large enough for the animals to move about freely. If Rabbits and Guinea Pigs are to be kept outside, the cages must be waterproof. Animals can stand cold, but not wet or draughts. Guinea Pigs and Rabbits need cages with a run and small enclosed sleeping place. Peat, coarse sawdust or newspaper can be used on the floor and changed frequently, and the bedding can be hay or dried leaves. (The children can collect leaves in the autumn and store them in boxes or sacks.) Both animals need water, dry food (baked bread, oats, cornflakes etc) and plenty of green food.

2 Hamsters, Mice and Gerbils can be kept in similar cages. Special wire ones can be bought, or perhaps there is a parent willing to make

pens. Shelves and ladders make the animals more interesting to watch and they get exercise moving on and off these. Mice and Hamsters are best with a fenced-off corner to keep the nest in place. Gerbils will make their own nest out of any materials given to them, and they will move it from place to place. All these animals can be fed on oats, cornflakes, hard baked bread, raisins etc and all need water. The Gerbils and Hamsters also like nuts, and pieces of apple and carrot.

WORKING AND RECORDING

If children are given the opportunity to watch animals they will be able to observe the main characteristics but they need to be made aware of what to look for. They will almost certainly have noticed the tail, the fur, the whiskers and, possibly, the colour. They will need to have the paws, claws, eyes, ears and teeth pointed out to them so that they can see how they differ from those of other animals. They can talk about the size, the shape, the way the animal moves, its colouring patterns and its food. The youngest children should be given plenty of opportunities to talk about animals, and to draw them.

Animals can be weighed. Very small ones, like Mice, can be put in a loosely closed paper bag for a few minutes; Rabbits and Guinea Pigs will usually sit still long enough in a scale pan; larger animals can be weighed on personal scales with a child holding them. The weight of the child can then be subtracted to obtain the animal's weight.

The length of an animal is usually measured from the nose to the tip of the tail. These measurements can be used to compare the size of animals and to show growth. Charts can be made of the measurements.

The children can write instructions for feeding or cleaning out their animals, e.g.

Feeding the Guinea Pig
Take the 2 dishes out of the cage.
Wash them.
Fill one with water.
Put one pot of food in the other.
(Keep the food in a box with a suitable small pot as a measure.)
Put them back into the cage.
Give it a carrot or some dandelions.

These notices can be part of the reading and writing work of the class, and so will serve several purposes.

Older children can do more definite work with the pets. They can be given cards setting out particular problems and be asked to solve them, e.g.

A Rabbit eats half its own weight in food every day. Could you eat half your weight in food?

The children will be quite certain they can do this, but they can weigh a small child, and then collect together half his weight in food. The results will certainly surprise them. The child concerned could be photographed with the food, and this could be used with a written account.

Examples of other problems are:

Can you find out how a Cat uses its whiskers?
How much food does the Mouse eat in a week?
How long does it take the Gerbils to chew up an egg box?
How far can the Mouse move in half a minute?

The Mouse can be put on a large sheet of paper, and its path can be chalked while one child watches a sand timer. The chalk line can be measured with string.

If a pair of animals is kept the babies can be studied from before birth until they are grown.

Various books and friezes can be made, e.g. 'Animal Pets', 'How to Look after the . . . ', 'Animal Ears', 'Animal Coverings', 'Baby Animals', 'The Baby Guinea Pig Book', 'Animals at the Zoo'.

All the animals are ideal stimuli for drawing, painting, collages, models and stitched pictures.

SUPPORT MATERIAL

Books for the children

Pets George Cansdale (Ladybird Books)
Guinea Pigs Rosemary Creele (Dinosaur Publications)
Rabbits Rosemary Creele (Dinosaur Publications)
Animal Homes Cathy Kilpatrick (Ward Lock)
Pets R.H.C. Fice and I.M. Simkiss (E.J. Arnold)

Books for teacher reference

A Field Guide to the Mammals of Britain and Northern Europe F.H. Van Den Brink (Collins)

Useful apparatus

Animal cages; small plastic bowls; balance; scales; tape measure; plastic bucket; small shovel; animal pictures.

11 PLAYING WITH MIRRORS

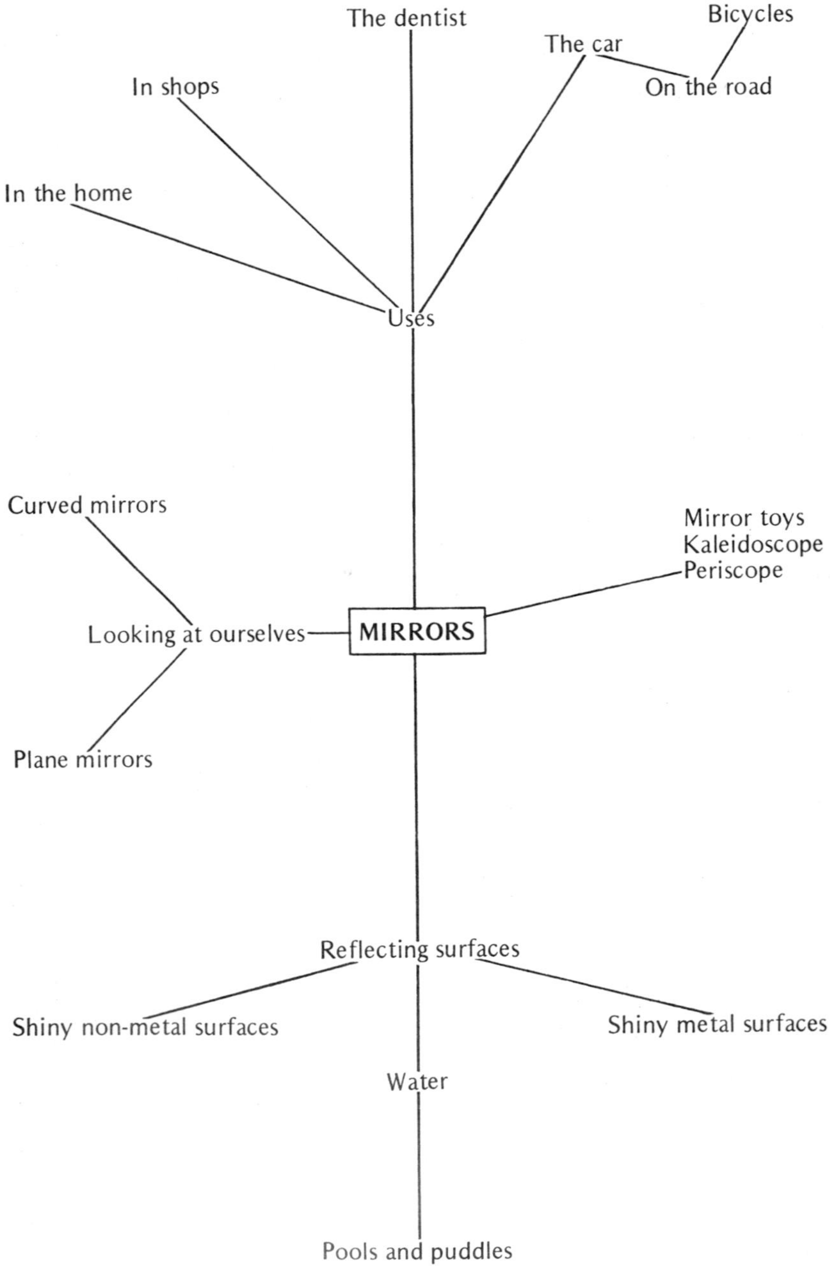

Small children are used to seeing themselves in mirrors, but they are too young to understand anything of the science of light. It is far better to let them play with mirrors, find reflective surfaces and discover some of the uses of these.

Most of the things that a young child finds out about the world around him are obtained by actual experience and, in the present day, he is surrounded by scientific discovery. Television, radio, cars, aeroplanes and electric light are all taken for granted, and playing with mirrors may seem a long way from the space rocket or the atomic submarine, but these very early experiences are the ones that become the foundations for later understanding.

GENERAL NOTES

1 Reflections can be seen wherever there is a smooth, shiny surface, e.g. glass and steel mirrors, tin cans, shiny spoons and knives, tiles, polished copper and brass, highly polished furniture, puddles and pools.

2 A flat mirror is called a plane mirror, and the image seen in it:

a is laterally inverted, i.e. it is changed from side to side — if you raise your right hand, the image in the mirror appears to raise its left hand ('mirror writing' is laterally-inverted writing)

b is the same size as the object that is being reflected

c looks as if it is as far behind the mirror as the object is in front of it.

3 Shiny, curved surfaces distort the image. In a convex mirror (such as the back of a spoon) the image is small, clear and the right way up. This makes it useful as a car mirror and a dentist's mirror. A concave mirror is one that is hollowed like the bowl of a spoon. When close to a concave mirror the image is large and the right way up. Shaving and make-up mirrors are usually concave.

4 Mirrors have many uses apart from the obvious one of reflecting our own image, e.g. a microscope with a mirror as a light reflector; a dentist's mirror; mirrors used on the road at blind corners; mirrors used to give an impression of space; distorting mirrors at fun-fairs; simple periscopes; mirrors placed to see the back of an exhibit in a museum.

5 If two mirrors are placed at an angle and an object is put between them, the number of images seen varies according to the size of the angle. If the mirrors are placed parallel to each other, and facing each other, any object inbetween them is reflected an infinite number of times.

6 As a plane mirror reflects an object exactly, symmetrical patterns can be shown. Half a man can be drawn on paper, and if the mirror is placed at the side the reflection in the mirror appears to complete the drawing. The drawing and the reflection are symmetrical.

'Mirror' symmetry can be found in many natural organisms, e.g. many leaves have one line of symmetry — that is they are more or less exactly the same on either side of the line of the main vein. Animals are symmetrical on either side of a line that divides the body into two.

PLANNING AND PREPARATION

1 A useful collection of materials for starting work on mirrors could include: small, real mirrors; steel mirrors; shiny tins; spoons; knives; a shiny metal jug or teapot; metal foil; shiny tiles; polished metal (brass, copper); dark glass bottle; shiny plastic objects etc. This could also include a dish of water.

2 Examples of the uses of mirrors could be collected:

a an ordinary, household mirror — as large as possible — for children to use when looking at their own reflections
b a make-up mirror
c a mirror used to put in a budgerigar's cage
d car mirrors (or pictures of cars showing the mirrors)
e Dentist's mirror (or picture of a dentist at work)
f ornamental objects using mirrors.

3 Collect shiny, curved surfaces so that children can see what happens when they look into these. There is no need for them to understand, at this stage, why the distortions occur.

4 A mirror is basically a sheet of glass with a backing. If small sheets of glass (with the edges taped) are collected, these can be used for experimenting. Children can try to make mirrors with backings of black or white paper, paint, metal foil or any other available materials.

5 A kaleidoscope is a toy with two or three mirrors inside a triangular tube. They can be bought quite cheaply from toy departments and are included in many of the catalogues of educational equipment firms. If you look through the kaleidoscope at, say, pieces of coloured plastic or paper, a regular pattern can be seen which changes every time the toy is moved slightly.

6 Holders for small mirrors can be made with Plasticine, or corks with slits cut in them can be used.

7 For simple experiments to show how mirrors can be used for looking round corners, a screen of some sort will be needed. A screen needs to be sufficiently high for a child sitting on one side of the table to be unable to see a child sitting on the other side of it. Using a mirror only the one child has to say what the other is putting on the table. Strong cardboard will make a screen and it can be held upright by tacking the bottom to a piece of wood.

8 Glass mirrors are undoubtedly the best and if handled carefully there will be no accidents. Edges can be bound with masking tape to eliminate any sharpness, and if the backs are taped at the same time, broken mirrors will not fall apart. Steel mirrors are expensive, but it is possible to buy plastic mirrors (see apparatus section at the end). These are quite satisfactory but they do scratch easily.

WORKING AND RECORDING

The youngest children can look at themselves in a large mirror. Ask them to find out if the reflection copies exactly what they do in front of it, and whether everything placed in front can be seen in the mirror. Give them instructions: 'Touch your eye. Touch your nose. Put your hands on your head.' Get them to give instructions to other children. Ask them what happens to the reflection in the mirror. Does it do the same things as the person in front of it?

Once they have looked at reflections they can be asked to find out if they can see their reflections in any other surfaces. Pictures of things with reflecting surfaces can be put into a book, or a collection of the things displayed. The children could also include things in which they cannot see a reflection. They can play with two mirrors, taped together at an angle, and see what happens to a toy car placed between the mirrors.

Older infants can try to make mirrors. If metal foil is smoothed with the fingers and then wrapped round a piece of card, can the children see their reflections in it ? By putting different backings on glass can they make mirrors? Examples can be displayed with notices explaining how the 'mirror' was made, and which experiment was the most successful.

If kaleidoscopes are available the children can draw some of the patterns they see in them. Older children will probably want to find out what is inside the kaleidoscope, and they could try and make one if two long mirrors are available. The third side can be made from stiff card, and all three taped together. This has the advantage that the children can put anything under it – pieces of wool, beads etc. Shop-bought kaleidoscopes are usually sealed.

Let children look at writing in the mirror. Ask them what has happened to it. Older infants can try to do mirror writing — so that when held in front of the mirror it is the right way round. They can make mirror-writing notices and ask their friends if they can read them, e.g.

Holding a mirror upright on a large sheet of paper, children can try to draw shapes — circles, squares and triangles — while looking in the mirror. One child can draw a pattern and ask a friend to copy it while looking in the mirror. Experiments can be devised to use mirrors for looking round corners etc. The children can be set simple problems to solve, e.g.

How can you use mirrors to see the back of your head?
Without turning round, can you find out what is on the table behind you?
Using the big mirror, can you put it so that you can see round the corner of the classroom (outside) while still standing by the door?
Can you make up a drawing game using a mirror?

Symmetry experiments can be tried. Start by giving the children a picture of, say, half a Butterfly and ask them to use the mirror to make the whole Butterfly. See if they can draw patterns which can be completed by placing the mirror on the line of symmetry. The patterns can be copied into their 'Mirror Books'.

Children can make books on 'Using Mirrors'. They can look around at home and school and find all the ways mirrors are used. This will, obviously, include similar examples but this does not matter. The main aim is to make them look around so that 'Doing my hair', 'Cleaning my teeth', 'Dad doing his hair', 'In a handbag' are all acceptable. Pictures (drawn or cut out) can be included. Similarly a book about surfaces that reflect could be put together. On a sunny day, or using the beam from a torch, children can reflect a spot of light from a mirror, and can try to answer some questions about this, e.g.

How far away can the spot be reflected?
Can it be shone into a shady or dark place?
Can the spot be made bigger or smaller?

SUPPORT MATERIAL

Books for the children

Mirrors and Patterns Romola Showell (Ward Lock Educational)

Books for teacher reference

Early Experiences Science 5/13 (Macdonald Educational)
Junior Science Source Book J.W. Bainbridge, R.W. Stockdale and E.R. Wastnedge (Collins)
General Science Book 4 Charles Windridge (Schofield & Sims)

Useful apparatus

Small glass mirrors; large mirror; steel and plastic mirrors; metal foil; metal spoons; tins; kaleidoscopes; make-up mirror.

Plastic mirrors (which can be cut with scissors) can be obtained from E.J. Arnold, Leeds. Plane and curved plastic mirrors are available.

12 COLOURS

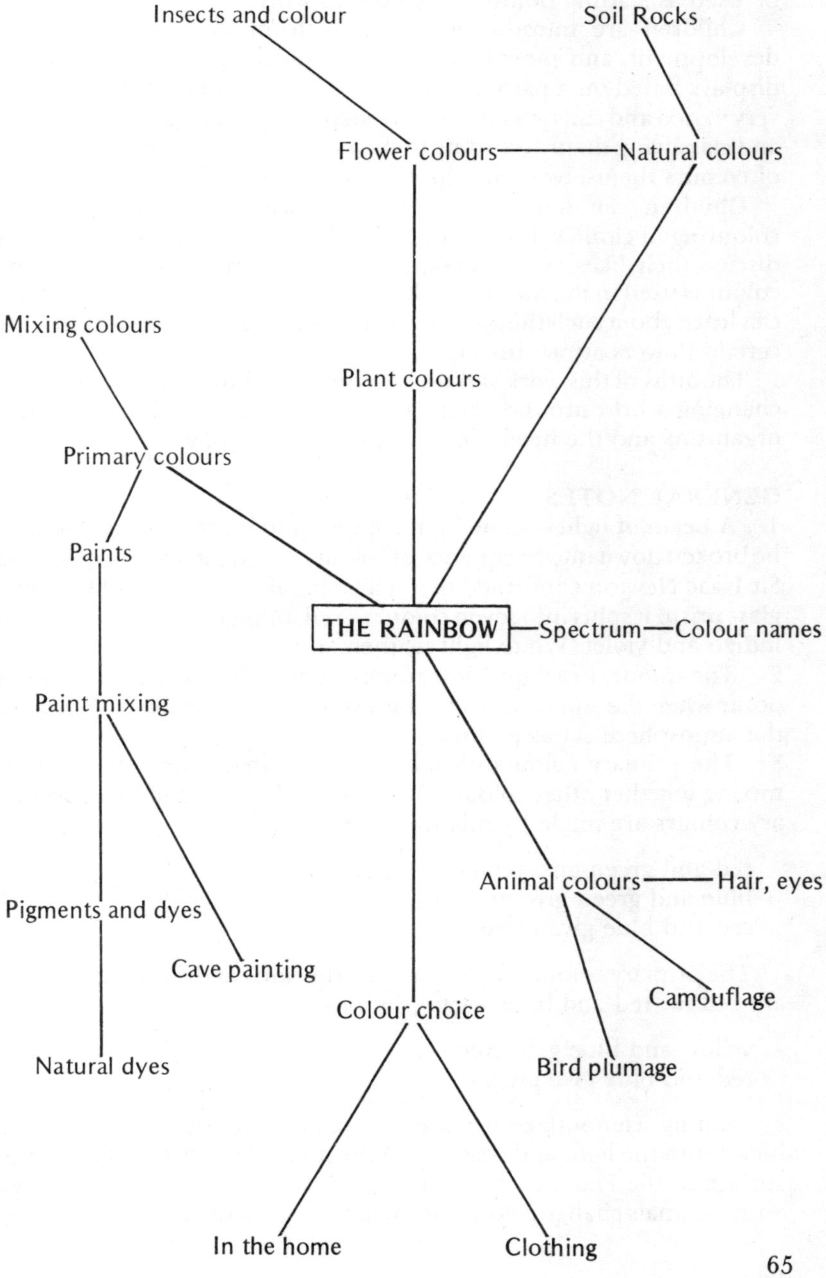

Insects and colour
Soil Rocks
Flower colours
Natural colours
Mixing colours
Plant colours
Primary colours
Paints
THE RAINBOW
Spectrum
Colour names
Paint mixing
Animal colours
Hair, eyes
Pigments and dyes
Cave painting
Colour choice
Camouflage
Natural dyes
Bird plumage
In the home
Clothing

Without colour the world around us would be far less interesting and attractive. We are used to seeing coloured objects, and the diversity of colour, and the vast number of shades of colour is worth considering on its own. Every classroom contains an abundance of material which can be used as starting points for children's work.

Children are introduced to colour from the earliest stages of development, and most infant teachers produce, from time to time, displays based on a particular colour. The work that could be done is very varied and can be as simple as looking at flowers, animals, birds etc and classifying them according to their colour, or a more detailed study of colours themselves, and the effects of mixing them.

Children can look at the colours around them and note the colouring of clothes, furnishings, hair, eyes, skin and plants. They can discuss their likes and dislikes, and they can find out ways in which colour is used in the home, at school and on the streets. Older children can learn about such things as animal camouflage, and the way in which certain flowers attract insects.

The aims of this work should be to give children an awareness of the changing world around them, the multiplicity of colour in natural organisms and the need for colour in our everyday lives.

GENERAL NOTES

1 A beam of light – white light – appears to be colourless, but it can be broken down into a sequence of colours called the spectrum. In 1666 Sir Isaac Newton confirmed that if a beam of light is passed through a glass prism it splits into seven colours – red, orange, yellow, green, blue, indigo and violet. White light is, then, a mixture of colours.

2 The colours in a rainbow are the same as in the spectrum. Rainbows occur when the sun shines after rain showers; raindrops suspended in the atmosphere act as prisms.

3 The primary colours of light are those that cannot be made by mixing together other colours. These are red, green and blue. Secondary colours are made by mixing these:

red and green give yellow
blue and green give turquoise
red and blue give crimson.

The primary colours of paint are not the same as those of light. These are yellow, red and blue. Again, by mixing,

yellow and blue give green
red and blue give purple

4 Animal camouflage depends on colour; the stripes of the Tiger blend with the light and shadows of the jungle, and the spotted upper-surface of the Plaice makes it almost invisible on the sandy sea-bed. Some animals change colour so that they blend into their surroundings.

Sometimes this change is fairly rapid (the Octopus and the Chameleon) and sometimes it is seasonal (the browny-red Stoat which changes in winter, in northern countries, to white). The Frog's skin will take on the colours of its habitat so that Frogs will vary from green to brown.

5 Among mammals only the primates (Man, Apes and Monkeys) can appreciate colour. Butterflies are probaby able to distinguish colours, but different species react to different ones. Bees are sensitive to certain colours, though apparently blind to red. Some people are colour blind. Their eyes are not sensitive to one or more of the primary colours. The commonest form of colour blindness is the inability to distinguish red and green.

6 Colours are all around us:

ourselves — skin, hair, eyes
plants — many greens, browns, flower colours
animal coverings — skin, hair, fur, scales, feathers, shells
yarn and fabrics — clothing, furnishings
stone and brick — buildings, walls
outdoor colours — rocks, sea, sky, plants
art and creative crafts.

7 Dyes are used to colour materials. These can be natural or chemical.

PLANNING AND PREPARATION

1 Collect together objects and materials for 'colour tables'. These will give the children some idea of the different shades of one colour that can be found. For example, a 'yellow table' might display yellow flowers, pieces of yarns and fabrics, clothing, crayons and paints, a banana, a lemon, toys, book covers, jewellery, pictures of cars, birds and butterflies, shells etc.

2 Classify colours in ways which children could use for further study:

colours and ourselves
flower colours
animal colours
colours I like
food colours
day and night colours.

3 Colour blending can be done with simple tops. Cut circles (about 4 cm radius) from thick, white card. These can be coloured in various ways, e.g. alternate segments of blue and yellow; concentric circles of blue and red; red and yellow spots. If a small pencil or a piece of dowel, sharpened at one end, is pushed through the centre, the top can be spun to show the effects of mixing the colours.

Colour tops

Bands of colour

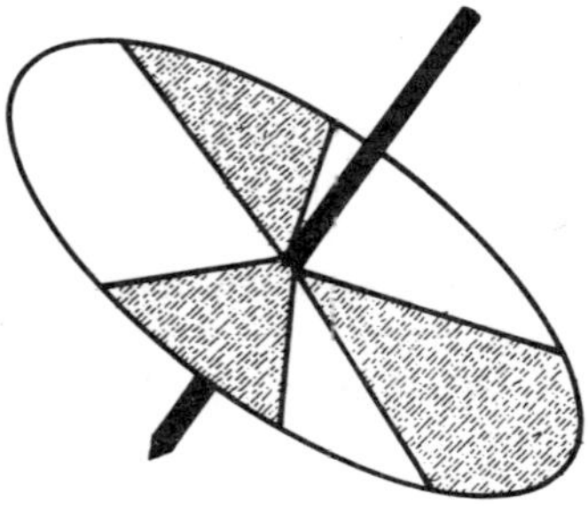

Segments of colour

4 Collect coloured transparent materials – sweet wrappings, glass, acetate, perspex etc. These can be placed over other colours to see the changes made. Toy spectacles can be made from card with coloured cellophane lenses. Children can try looking through these.
5 Light can be shone through a prism to show the composition of the spectrum. A simple way to make a rainbow, or spectrum, is to put a clear tumbler, full to the top with water, on a window sill in bright sunlight. If the tumbler is put on the edge of the sill, a 'rainbow' will appear on a piece of white paper placed on the floor.
6 Collect pieces of fabric or wallpaper with definite patterns (stripes, spots, florals). Make cut-out animal silhouettes from white paper, and ask the children to 'camouflage' them so that they will look like the background. Following this children could look further at animal and military camouflage.
7 Consider colour change as an approach to this work:

leaves changing from green to brown, in autumn
colours fading in sunlight
colour changes in the sky
dyeing materials
fruit ripening
colour changes during cooking
changes in the landscape between winter and summer.

8 Note examples of the definite use of colour:

traffic lights
coloured wires (for connecting to electric plugs)
street signs

red as a danger signal
colour in art.

9 Tie-dyeing can be used to show colour change, and the use of colour. This activity always interests children, particularly if they dye a piece of material that can be made into something afterwards. This is now a fairly common school craft, and most people know how to set about it. With young children use cold-water dyes, and see that they make the ties tight enough. Rubber bands are the easiest thing to use, but pieces of wool and string are just as good. Results are best if the material is dyed, rinsed, opened out and left to dry before dyeing with a second colour. Very young children cannot manage the tying successfully, but good results can be obtained using polythene bags. Screw up a piece of material (washed sheeting gives good results) and put it into a polythene bag. Pull the bag tight and seal the opening with a rubber band. Put this bundle into another bag and seal again. Prick the bundle all over with an ordinary pin, but do not tear the polythene. Put the whole package into the dye and leave for fifteen minutes. Rinse well before opening the bags. The patterns made are very attractive, but a dark dye is needed.

10 Children can try dyeing with natural dyes, e.g. material boiled with onion skins to give a yellow colour. They can try things that they suggest themselves — Oak leaves, Blackberries, Lichen, bark, grass etc.

WORKING AND RECORDING

The youngest children can collect coloured things, and can try to decide which is the commonest colour. They can make charts of colours they like and dislike, and can make pictures or dress a doll in the colours they like. They can look at themselves and the other children in the class, and could then make a hair-colour frieze.

Ordinary school powder paints can be used for experiments with colour mixing. If jars of paint are made up the children can experiment with different mixtures. If this mixing is done using a plastic teaspoon the children can see the results of a definite experiment. If they put a teaspoonful of red in a saucer and then add one spoonful of blue they can record the work by painting strips on paper — a red strip, a blue strip and then a strip showing the mixture. Alternatively they could shake up mixtures of colours in small, transparent bottles, and label each bottle to indicate the mixture.

Problem cards could be made setting out possible experiments for them to do, e.g.

Get pots of red, blue and yellow paint.
If you use two of these paints, can you make green?
Write it down like this:
. . . and . . . make green.

Can you make brown?
Can you make orange?
Can you make purple?

Children can experiment with colour. They can paint pictures of animals to blend in with backgrounds (these can be pieces of material, pictures already painted of trees etc) and they can make model rooms from shoe boxes and paint the walls and doors in ways that please them. Dolls house furniture can be put into the rooms to make them look more realistic.

They can make colour-blending tops, deciding on the colours and patterns themselves. These tops could be displayed, and each child could explain what happened when he spun his own top.

If flower colours are looked at the children can decide which is the commonest colour, and which colours insects seem to prefer. If there is no access to growing flowers, pieces of brightly coloured paper can be put outside on a warm, sunny day (when flies etc are likely to be around) and they can watch to see which colour the insects alight on. They can keep a record of the results.

Older children can experiment with visibility. If a piece of card is fixed upright, coloured toy cars can be placed by it. The children can move some distance away and then decide which car is the easiest to see, e.g. a black background with toy cars (or bricks) in yellow, red, dark blue, white, black, green etc.

A survey can be made of street colours and pictures made to show what the children have seen. They may notice red letter-boxes, red and black street signs, traffic lights, green lamp posts etc.

Painting materials can be explored. Tell older children that they are going to paint pictures but that they cannot use any of their usual paints. There could be some discussion about cave paintings, and ask the children to suggest how primitive man could have painted pictures without paint. Some of the materials they might think of are soil and water mixed together, blood, grass, squashed flower petals, burnt wood etc.

They could make picture and information books about one colour and make collections of wools, fabrics, wallpaper, coloured papers, toys etc to show the vast variety of colours. They could also be asked to make suggestions themselves for further work.

Material can be dyed, and experiments made to see if one colour can be changed to another. Can white material be dyed any colour? Can green material be dyed yellow? Is it possible to dye black material? Half the fun of tie-dyeing is opening out the results.

The work that is possible, using colour as the basis, is endless, and much of it can be done while studying other topics. The children could, for example, look at bird colouring while doing a project on birds seen at the local zoo. Most of the recording can be done with pictures and charts and the results of experiments displayed together with short explanations of how the work was carried out.

SUPPORT MATERIAL

Books for the children

Rainbow Colours Starters Series (Macdonald Educational)
Light and Colour First Library Series (Macdonald Educational)

Books for teacher reference

Coloured Things Science 5/13 (Macdonald Educational)
The Use of Vegetable Dyes V. Thurstan (Dryad Press)
General Science Book 4 Charles Windridge (Schofield & Sims)

Useful apparatus

Coloured wools; fabrics; papers of all kinds; small pots; paint brushes; transparent materials; torch; glass prism; cardboard tops; crayons; paints; pictures of cars; animals; birds; fish etc.

13 TIME THINGS

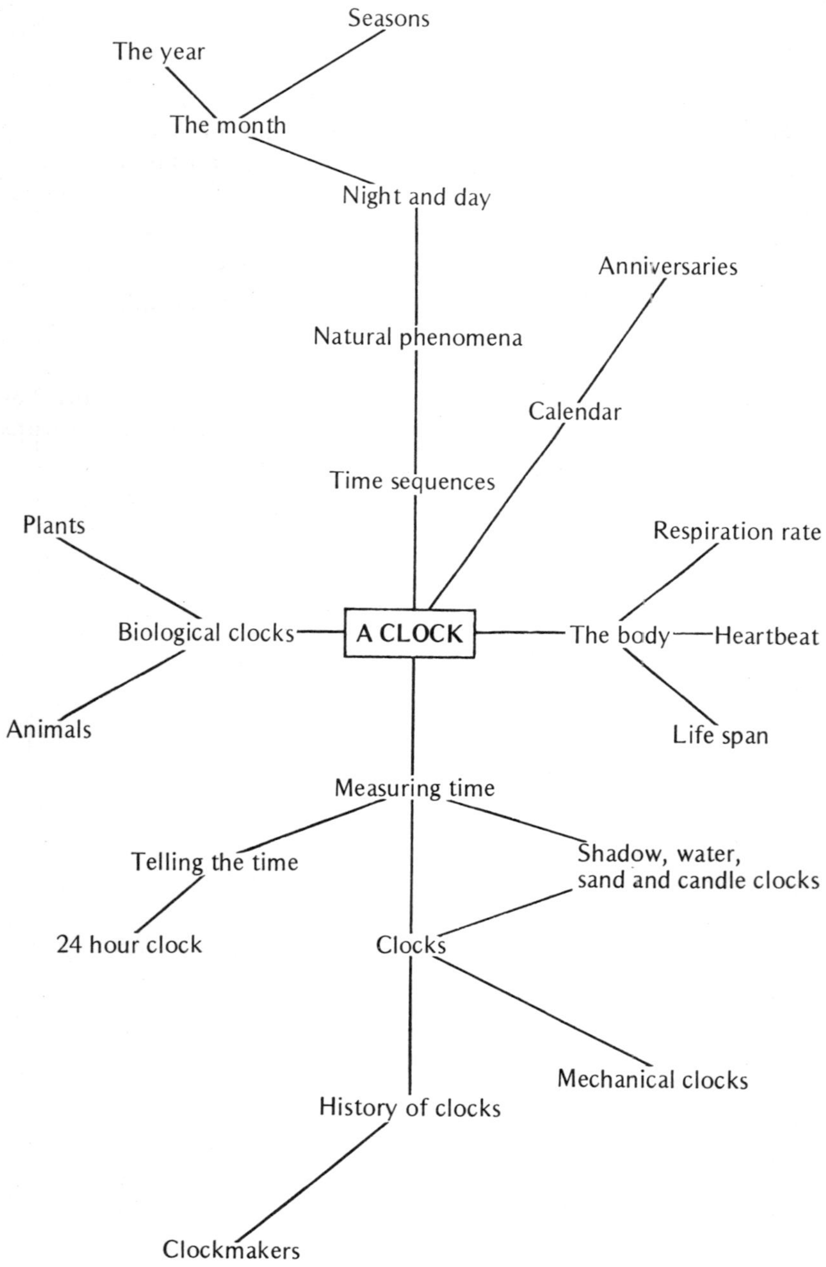

Young children gradually become aware of units of time because of the regular events that take place; they get up in the morning and go to bed at night; at midday they have their dinner; once a week they go to grandma's to tea. Passage of time is measured by the sequence of happenings within a given period — get up, have breakfast, go to school, have milk etc.

At a fairly early age they notice that watches and clocks are used by people to 'tell the time', and they accept these conventional timers as a part of everyday life, but it is possible for them to use other timing devices to indicate the interim between two events, e.g. candle and water clocks, sand timers etc.

To the youngest children a birthday is a pleasant day with the possibility of presents and cards. They have no idea that it is an anniversary of an event that tôok place three, four, five or six years ago. A year is an impossibly long unit of time, and difficult for them to comprehend; it is equally difficult for an adult to envisage that the first dinosaurs appeared on earth some 200,000,000 years ago!

After doing some of the work suggested, the children should have a clearer concept of time, should have begun to understand the sequencing of events in any day, and should have sufficient knowledge to use simple timers.

GENERAL NOTES

1 Early man must have judged time from the recurrence of night and day, and the changing seasons. Perhaps he also noticed that the moon changed shape regularly, and that the sun appeared to move across the sky. Also, the ebb and flow of the tide occurred regularly and rhythmically.

2 The length of a day (twenty-four hours) is the time taken for the earth to rotate on its own axis, and as the sun cannot be overhead in all places at once, time varies round the globe. World time is all related to Greenwich Mean Time. A month approximates to the time taken for the moon to move around the earth — this is about 29½ days. A year is the time taken by the earth to travel round the sun, and this takes 365 days 5 hours 48 minutes and 46 seconds. This is obviously an inconvenient length of time and so a year is considered to be 365 days long, and an extra day is added every four years to account for the odd hours. A day is deemed to begin at midnight. The first twelve hours are designated a.m. (*ante meridiem* — before noon) and the next twelve hours p.m. (*post meridiem* – after noon). To avoid errors a twenty-four-hour clock can be used, e.g.

12.00 midnight	0000
2.00 a.m.	0200
12.00 noon	1200
2.00 p.m.	1400
6.00 p.m.	1800

3 Clocks are very old. The ancient Egyptians used shadow and candle clocks and the earliest known sundial is believed to have been made over 3000 years ago. Water clocks (clepsydra) are probably as old as shadow clocks, and did not have to rely on the sun shining. Sand and candle clocks were used to indicate definite passages of time, so a timer might take one hour for the sand to run through, or the candle clock could be marked in such a way that the candle burnt down to a mark at the end of every hour. It is not known who invented the first mechanical clock but they all contain three main parts:

the driving mechanism — this may be a falling weight, a spring or an electric motor
the regulating mechanism — which ensures that the clock keeps time — this may be a pendulum or a balance spring
the escapement — which links the driving mechanism and the regulating mechanism and governs the speed of rotation of the wheel moving the hands on the clock face.

It is probable that the first clocks had no hands at all but just struck the hours and quarters. The history of clocks makes an interesting study in itself, and will introduce children to such people as Galileo, Robert Hooke, Thomas Tompion and Robert Harrison.

4 Historical time is very difficult for young children to understand. They often find it impossible to cope with the idea of time passing during one day and last year means no more to them than yesterday. It is often easier to start from the present and work backwards, increasing the spaces between events as the child gets older and is more able to comprehend the passage of days, weeks, months and years.

5 Biological clocks — or the regular actions of plants and animals — can be studied, e.g.

the opening and shutting of flowers (the Daisy is a good example for children)
bird migration
alteration of colour according to season, and alteration in the thickness of animal fur and hair
roosting of birds at night
waking at dusk of night-active animals
nest building activities in spring
appearance of frog spawn in spring
leaf fall in autumn.

6 There are many time words which could be used to start a project:

second	spring	calendar	present
minute	summer	clock	future
hour	autumn	timer	a.m.

day	winter	sundial	p.m.
week	season	watch	BC
month	today	decade	AD
year	tomorrow	era	
fortnight	yesterday	lifetime	
century	night	past	

PLANNING AND PREPARATION

1 Pendulums can be made with weights hung on string. If the length of the string is altered it can be seen that the pendulum will swing at a different rate — the shorter the string the greater number of times the pendulum will swing in a minute. One swing is counted when the pendulum swings forward and back to the start. If a washing-up liquid bottle is cleaned and thoroughly dried it can be filled with salt, and suspended upside down. As it swings (as a pendulum) the salt will trace out patterns onto a sheet of black paper underneath.

2 A sand timer can be made using a washing-up liquid bottle, filled with salt, and inverted over a narrow glass jar. As it would be impractical to graduate this using natural phenomena, such as midday to midday, it will be necessary to use an ordinary clock to mark the jar. It can, of course, be used as an arbitrary timer. A line can be marked on the jar, and children can use it for timing definite actions, e.g. how many bricks can I drop in the box while the timer fills up to the red line? Fine sand can be used for these timers, but this is not always easy to get.

3 Water clocks can be made in various ways:

a A small hole can be made in the bottom of a plastic bottle. The water will drip out of this, and the timing can be done either by letting the bottle drip until empty, or by letting it drip into a graduated jar.

b A plastic basin, with a hole in the bottom, can be floated in a large bowl of water. Water will go into the basin through the hole, and graduation lines can be marked on the sides of the basin. The basin needs weighting slightly with Plasticine to keep it floating level.

c Cut the top off a large plastic bottle so that you can see inside it easily. Make a small hole in the bottom, and fill the bottle with water. Float a cork on the top. As the water drips out the water level will go down, taking the cork with it. The position of the cork can be used to indicate a space of time.

4 Candle clocks will need supervision, but children enjoy them. A candle can be marked by tying thread round it, or by sticking pins into it. The graduations can either indicate definite times (e.g. it will burn for thirty minutes between each graduation) or it can be used as an arbitrary timer.

A candle clock

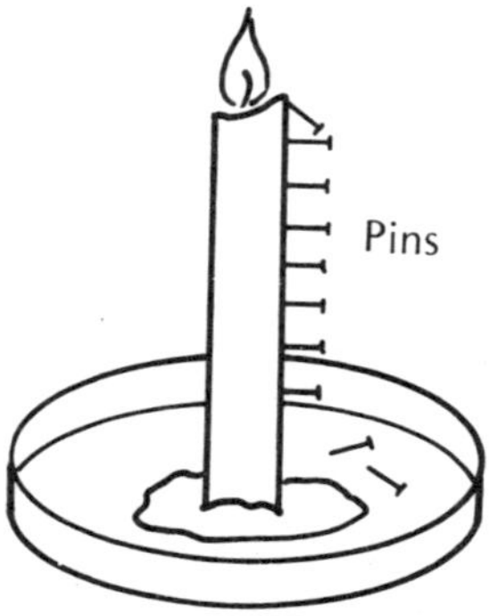

Candle in Plasticine fixed to a tin lid.

If a fairly accurate result is wanted keep the candle away from draughts. A candle alarm clock can be made by tying a length of cotton round the candle. If the cotton is allowed to dangle over the edge of a table a nail can be tied to the end, and a tin lid placed on the floor under this. When the candle burns down to the cotton this will break and the nail will drop onto the tin lid.

5 Shadow clocks can be used outside on sunny days. The simplest is a length of dowel pushed into a flower pot filled with sand or stones. The position of the shadow can be chalked on the ground every hour. If this can be done for several days the children can see that the position of the shadow is the same for a particular time each day. Older children can look at a real sundial (or a picture of one) and can try to decide why this type of clock has very limited use. Quite often it takes them a long time to realize that the sundial could not be used at night!

6 Older children could try timing with their own pulse beats. Children usually find it hard to feel the pulse, but if a drawing pin is pushed into a drinking straw (so that the straw is horizontal) and the head of the drawing pin is placed over the wrist pulse, the straw will move as the pulse beats.

7 A large-faced stop clock is useful for time work, and there are several commercially-produced sand timers and rocker timers which can be bought quite cheaply. Children do not need to be able to tell the time to use the stop clock. They can either be told that 'it takes a minute for the hand to move all round the clock' or they can use it to count actions 'while the hand goes round once'.

WORKING AND RECORDING

The youngest children can be given cards which they have to put into sequence. These cards should have pictures on them which show, clearly, actions that the children will recognize, e.g. a child getting out of bed, putting clothes on, eating breakfast, walking to school, having tea, going to bed etc.

They can use a simple sand timer to time certain actions, and some of these need not involve counting, e.g. While the sand runs through . . .

How many bricks can you put into the box? (counting)
How many bricks can you put in a line? (no counting — measure one line against another)
How much water can you put in the jar using this spoon? (no counting)
How many times can you jump? (counting)
Who can walk the furthest? (no counting)

Time words can be introduced orally. What did we do yesterday? Where did we go this morning? Who is going to play with the cars after dinner?

A day chart can be made showing what the children have done all day (in the correct order). They can illustrate it with pictures. They can also make a week chart which shows special happenings on days of the week. This will also introduce them to the names of the days, and the order in which they occur.

Older infants can make some of the simple timers and can use these to time actions. They can explain how they made their timers, and can make charts to indicate what they were used for, e.g.

I used my sand timer.
While the salt ran to the red line on the jar I
 bounced my ball 11 times
 counted to 23
 wrote my name 1 time
 put 16 beads in a pot
 walked 12 steps.

A clock exhibition could be arranged. Children can bring old clocks and watches, and these can be augmented with pictures to show as many different types of clock as possible. Books could be borrowed from the local library to show some of the very old clocks, and children could make pictures of any clocks they have seen in the neighbourhood (on the church tower; at the local garage; outside the bank etc).

The children can make birthday charts. If twelve envelopes (with flaps folded back) are stuck onto card the months can be written on them. Each child can write his name on a small card and can put it in the envelope showing his birthday month. A question card can be made to go with this, e.g.

Which envelope has the most cards? Which month has the most birthdays? Are there any months with no birthdays? Who has a birthday near Christmas (in December)? How many boys have birthdays in May?

The older children can be given workcards setting out particular problems to do with time, e.g.

a If there were no clocks in the world, could you tell the time?
   Could you tell if it was time to go to bed?
   Could you tell if it was dinner time?
   How could you tell?
b Every day the tide goes in and out.
   Every day the starlings come into the town for the night.
   Can you find some other things that happen every day?
c Make an 'Everyday Book'.
   Put in it all the things you do every day.
   Put them in the right order.

With a stop clock the children can do some accurate timing. They could, for example, find out how far a Snail walks in one minute. (Put the Snail on a sheet of paper and chalk its track. Measure the chalk line with string.) They could find out how long it takes them to walk to school or how many times they can step on and off a chair in a minute. The children will be able to think out problems for themselves, and all their work can be recorded either orally or written in a 'Book About Time'.

SUPPORT MATERIAL

Books for the children

Time, Calendars and Clocks Roy Worvill (Ladybird Books)
Time Denis Wrigley (Lutterworth Press)
Time Things Romola Showell (Ward Lock Educational)
Time E. Ramsbottom and J. Redmayne (Macmillan Education)

Books for teacher reference

Sciencewise Book 2 (Teachers' Book) Sheila Parker and Alan Ward (Nelson)
Time Stages 1 and 2 Science 5/13 (Macdonald Educational)
Work cards
Time Frank Briggs (Macmillan Education) (This is a set of 30 work cards and a Teachers' Guide)

Useful apparatus

Plastic bottles; jam jars; pins; candles; thread; flower pots; dowel; envelopes; thick and thin card; corks; washing-up liquid bottles; nails; string; small weights or large washers; tin lids; Alka-seltzer bottles; table salt; chalk; old clock; pictures of clocks and watches.

14 WHEELS

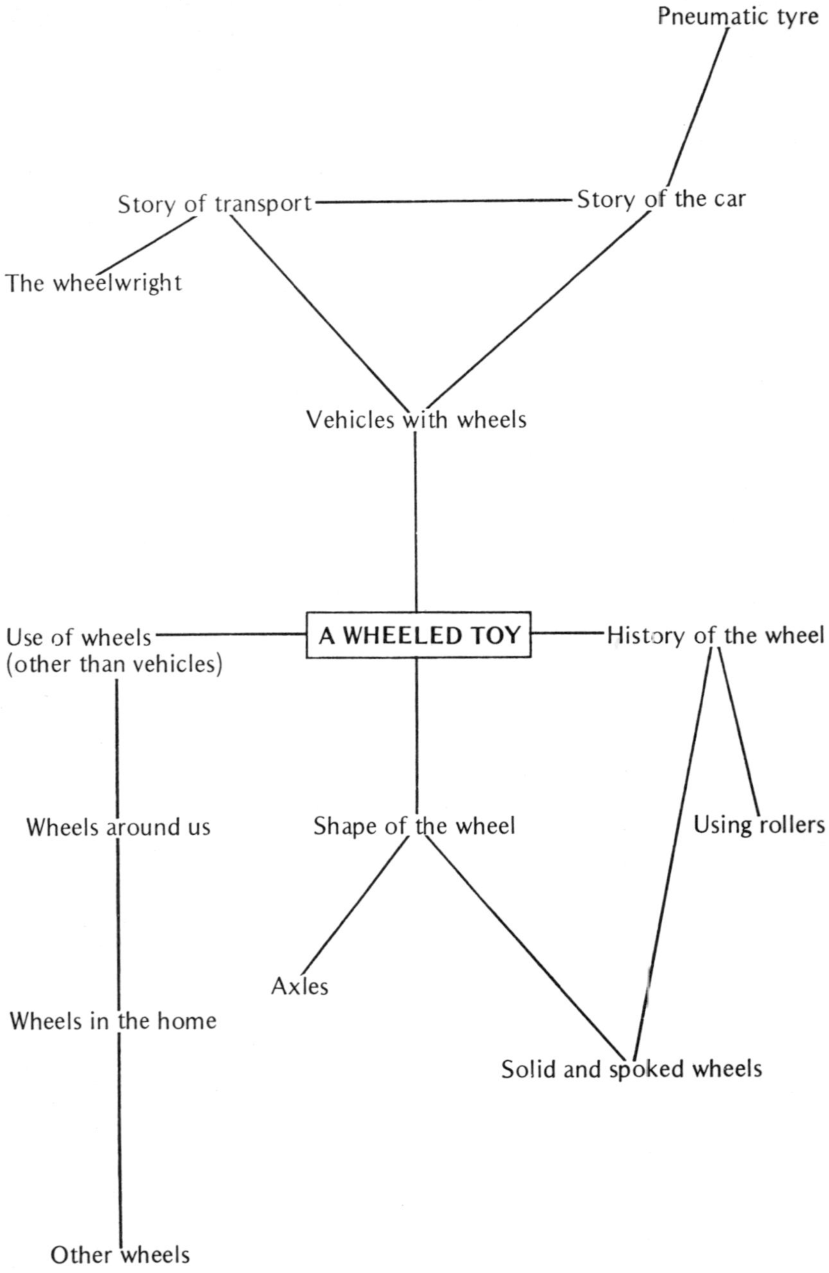

Pneumatic tyre
Story of transport
Story of the car
The wheelwright
Vehicles with wheels
Use of wheels
(other than vehicles)
A WHEELED TOY
History of the wheel
Wheels around us
Shape of the wheel
Using rollers
Axles
Wheels in the home
Solid and spoked wheels
Other wheels

With young children it is almost impossible to isolate science topics, and most of the projects undertaken will involve mathematics, history, art, craft or creative writing. The story of the wheel makes a fascinating history topic, but it can also be the start of work on transport, movement and tools.

Everyday the child will see wheels of some sort. These may be on cars, buses, bicycles, prams or on toys, but the child will recognize them. Without consciously noticing it he will have realized that they are, basically, all the same shape and perform similar functions.

Less obvious uses of wheels are still to be found in every home — in fact, everywhere we go. Wheels can be found in watches and clocks (cog wheels), on the sewing machine, inside the car (steering wheel), used as pulleys, as parts of tools (a hand-drill or an egg whisk) etc. It is difficult to imagine what our lives would be like without the wheel, and the story of the wheel can be approached from this angle. Older children may have visited or seen films about Stonehenge and can discuss how these enormous stones could have been moved without the aid of modern machinery. They may also have done some work about Stone Age people and could try and work out ways in which they could have moved large objects (logs, stones, dead animals).

They could also consider specialized uses of wheels and, if possible, see these working. For example, the potter's wheel and the windmill. The work of the wheelwright has been of considerable importance historically, and some fine examples of work done in the past can be seen in museums — particularly those housing exhibits of agricultural machinery.

This is a topic which could be undertaken with children of any age. Wheels can be seen everywhere and the work can be geared to suit the particular class.

GENERAL NOTES

1 The wheel was probably man's first invention. Before this rollers were almost certainly used. These would have been round, reasonably smooth logs, and could have been used to move very heavy weights. Obviously this involved a considerable number of people — cutting the rollers, hauling the weight, and moving the back rollers to the front as the load passed over them. The eighty or so largest stones (the Sarsens) at Stonehenge must have been dragged in this way from the Marlborough Downs to the present site.

2 The stages at which man began to use the wheel varied from place to place. It is believed that the Sumerians were the first people to use a cart wheel, possibly as early as 3000 BC. From Homer's *Iliad* we learn that spoked wheels were being used by the Greeks during the siege of Troy and many pictures on pottery and walls show spoked wheels on chariots dating from about 1400 BC. In Britain it is thought that the wheel was not used before 500 BC, and that it was probably brought here by

invaders.

3 Other historically useful wheels were the potter's wheel, the water wheel, the spinning wheel and the windmill. The mechanical clock was first devised in the thirteenth century and depended on the use of wheels.

4 As passenger transport developed the wheel improved. By the early seventeenth century coaches were in regular use and in 1784 light-weight mail coaches were introduced. The bicycle dates from the beginning of the nineteenth century, and the first were propelled along by pushing on the ground with the feet.

5 The history of the railways is a topic in itself and there are many books on the subject. The same applies to the history of the car, and with this comes the story of the pneumatic tyre. It is fascinating to note that the story goes from Sumeria in 3000 BC to the present day, and from solid wooden wheels to those capable of carrying Concorde.

PLANNING AND PREPARATION

1 Using rollers

You will need a stout wooden box (large enough for a small child to sit in) and rollers made from pieces of broom handles, or other round wooden poles. One child sits in the box and the other children can try to push or pull it along. After this the box can be put on the rollers, and the same thing tried. The back roller will have to be moved to the front as the box passes over it.

2 The shape of wheels

Children will know that wheels are circular, but they can experiment to see what would happen if wheels were any other shape. Thick card 'wheels' can be put on boxes, using brass paperclips as axles. If these are not circular, but elliptical, square, rectangular, triangular or hexagonal they can push the boxes along, and see which move the most easily.

3 Axles

The axle is at the centre of the wheel, but children can find out what happens if this is not so. Round wheels can be cut from thick card and the paperclip axles used for attaching them to boxes can be placed anywhere, except in the centre.

4 Pulleys

A very simple pulley can be made with a cotton reel. A wire loop is passed through the hole (wire coat hangers can be cut up for this) and this can be hung on a hook. The reel can then be used as a pulley and children can pull up small loads with this. In practice it is really better to use a real pulley. Meccano make a pulley set which can be used for experiments. Children can find out that it is easier to raise a bucket of water using a pulley than it is just using a rope passed over a bar.

5 Other models

a A simple water wheel can be made using a cork with blades made from pieces of plastic pushed into slots. If a hole has been made through the centre, the wheel will turn round a steel knitting needle when water drips on the blades.

b A windmill can be made from a square of stiff paper (see diagram below). Cut along the lines. Take all corners marked X to the middle and glue them to the middle. Attach a small stick (or pencil) with a drawing pin. This works better if a bead is placed between the windmill and the stick.

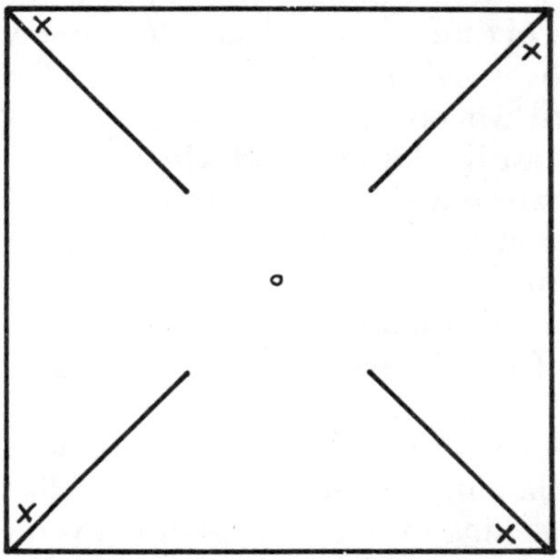

c Colour wheels are thick round cards made into tops with a piece of pencil pushed through the middle (see page 67–8).

A set of plastic Meccano is very useful for model making.

WORKING AND RECORDING

Work about wheels can vary from very simple projects to reasonably complicated topics. The youngest children can talk about all the different wheels they see, and can draw pictures of these or make a scrap book from cut-out pictures, including pictures of:

cars, lorries, vans and buses
bicycles and tricycles
prams, trolleys, wheelbarrows etc
trains, aeroplanes, road rollers
spinning wheel, sewing machine, potter's wheel, tools etc
cog wheels of different sorts.

A display can be made of all the toys the children can find which have wheels. With older children the display can include anything that they can collect which has a wheel or wheels. They may need to be reminded that a wheel can be found in less obvious places, e.g. inside a watch, a measuring wheel, the steering wheel of a car, the gear wheels of a bicycle, castors on furniture.

Models can be made to show why wheels need to be round and why the axles need to be in the middle. Pulleys, water wheels, cars and barrows etc can also be modelled and written work can be done to explain how they were made.

Older infants can do some mathematics connected with wheels. They can use a measuring wheel to find the length of the playground or school hall, and they can check that the circumference of the wheel is what is written on the label. They can measure round a bicycle wheel and find out how far the bicycle will travel if the wheel goes round a certain number of times, or can decide how many times it would have to go round to cover a given length. If they can look at cars they could measure standard wheels and mini wheels, and discuss which set of tyres is likely to last the longest and why.

If cog wheels are put together in groups of three or more and are turned, the children can look at the direction of turn of each wheel and can draw diagrams of these.

Books can be made on definite topics, e.g. 'The Story of the Wheel', 'A Scrap Book of Cars', 'The Story of the Car', 'The Story of Road Travel'.

A frieze on the history of the wheel could be accompanied by a taped commentary explaining the pictures. Children like making tapes once they are used to talking into a microphone. Even very young children can be taught to use a tape recorder.

Slides and tapes can be used together. There are many commercially produced slides of cars, coaches, carriages etc or you can take your own photographs, and the tape could include a commentary, suitable street noises or a musical background. Obviously young children could not produce such a programme themselves, but they could help to put it together, and could discuss content.

SUPPORT MATERIAL

Books for the children

Wheels Starters Series (Macdonald Educational)
The Wheel Denis Wrigley (Lutterworth Press)
The Story of the Bicycle Edmund Hunter (Ladybird Books)
Man and his Car James Webster (Ladybird Books)
The Motor Car Eileen Harries (Macdonald Educational)

Books for teacher reference

Sciencewise Book 2 (Teachers' Book) Sheila Parker and Alan Ward (Nelson)
Infant Handwork Isobel Arneil (Nelson)
Junior Handwork Isobel Arneil (Nelson)
Transport Edward Hayward (Macdonald Educational)

Useful apparatus

Thick card; cotton reels; wire; string; paper clips; assortment of cardboard boxes; a wooden box; broom handles; old clock; pulleys; set of plastic Meccano; wheeled toys.

15 TOOLS AND MACHINES

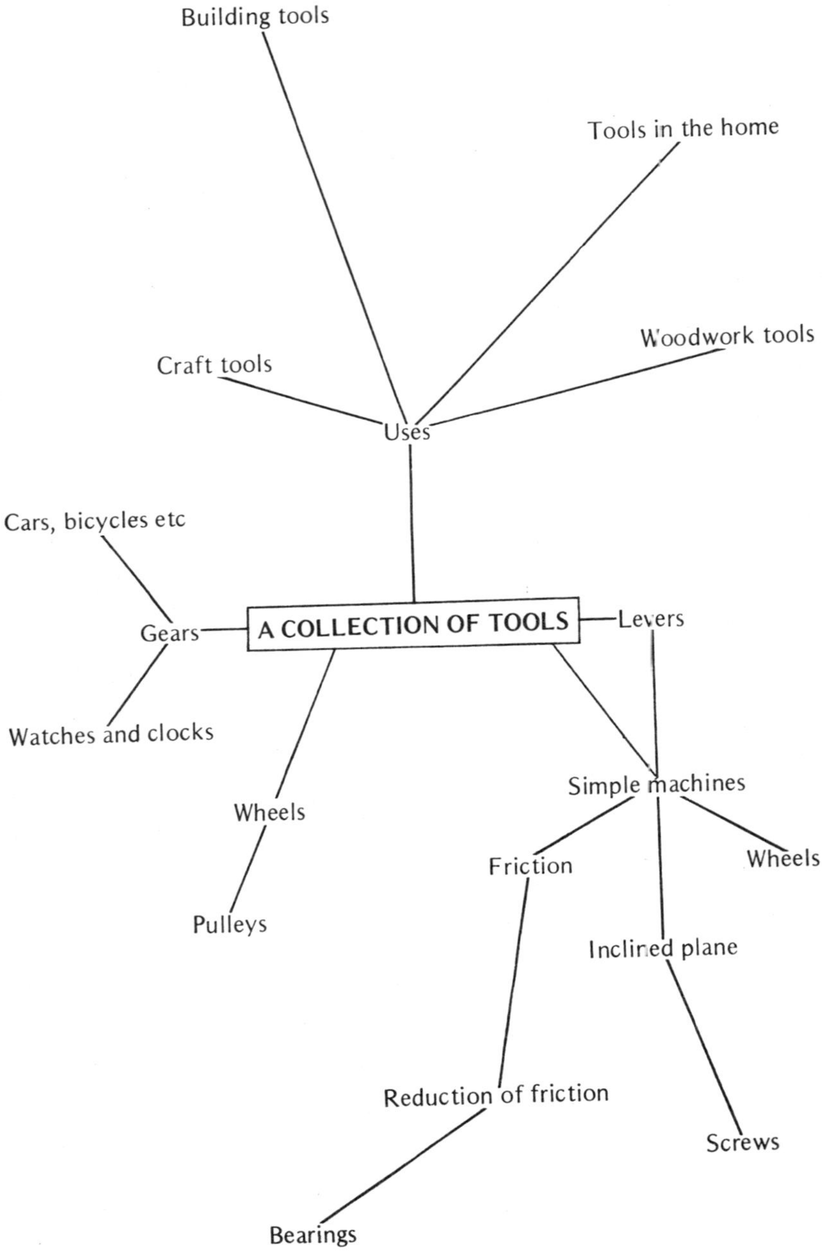

Man appears to have been a tool user from prehistoric times. His first tools were simple ones made of stone, bone or stick, but as he learnt how to handle metals the tools improved, but however a tool is used or made its basic function is to make a particular job easier.

The first tools needed must have been for hunting animals for food and for their skins. The animals must have been killed, skinned, cut up and the hides used for clothing. All these tasks would have been very difficult using only the hands and tools must have been essential for survival.

When man began to keep animals and to grow crops other tools were needed, and weapons were developed so that he could defend himself against marauders.

Children are accustomed to using tools though they may not realize that they are doing so. Almost the first tool that a child will learn to handle is a spoon, and he quickly learns to use such things as a pencil or a simple digging tool. He pushes his toy truck round the room on its wheels — these are tools — and he sees people using hammers, needles, tin-openers, scissors etc. As he develops he learns to use more and more complex tools and may, eventually, use the specialized tools of a particular craft or trade.

Those tools designed for specific jobs can be looked at, and it is often possible to get an expert into school to show children how certain tools are used, e.g. a carpenter using the commoner woodwork tools, a caneworker making a basket, a spinner or weaver demonstrating his craft.

Whatever work is done the children should be given the opportunity to see how tools are used, why they are used and, where possible, to handle them for themselves. They should look at the very wide variety of tools and should be able to see that a tool can be as simple as a needle or as technically complicated as a typewriter. (This is keeping the range of tools within the possibility of the children actually seeing them and handling them.)

They should also be able to realize that machines make work easier. They are used for doing work more efficiently, for moving things with the minimum of effort, and for producing the millions of components that are part of everyday living.

GENERAL NOTES

1 The history of tools would make a worthwhile study in itself — starting from the Stone Age and ending with the present day. Stone Age man must have used hammers, axes, knives and hand-ploughs made out of stone, but these had limitations which were never really overcome until he learnt to use metals. Children, considering primitive man, could discuss the tools he must have used, though it is obviously impossible for the youngest children to appreciate how far back in time this takes us. They will probably understand little of the time scale, but

can play a 'let's pretend' game of imagining that they were going to live on an island with no houses, shops, cars etc. Some of the tools they could consider are:

stones used as hammers
stones sharpened (by hitting with other stones) to make axes, scrapers for hides and knives for cutting up and skinning animals
shoulder-blade bones for digging the ground
sticks sharpened (by rubbing them on stone) to make spears for hunting
heavy pieces of wood as weapons
round branches used as rollers
pieces of bone used as needles to make holes in hides so that they could be stitched together with strips of hide.

2 One of the simplest tools is the lever. When we get a lid off a tin using the spoon handle we are using a lever; raising something with a pole pivoted across a stone is also an example of a lever. The pivot is called the fulcrum and the lever is supported at this point. Using a lever less effort is needed and work becomes easier. Scissors are double levers with the fulcrum at the point where the two blades are joined. A seesaw is an example of the simplest lever. If the children on it are positioned properly it is possible for a heavy child to be lifted into the air by a much lighter child (the heavy child has to be nearer to the centre than the lighter one). Other examples of levers are garden shears, nutcrackers, a wheelbarrow, and oars when a boat is being rowed.

3 The wheel is one of the most important tools, and wheels and levers form the working parts of many machines. Pulleys are wheeled tools used for lessening the effort of lifting or hauling (see Section 14 *Wheels*).

4 One of the simplest machines is the inclined plane. This is simply a slope for raising loads from one level to another with less effort. A ramp is an inclined plane, and it is obviously far easier to raise, say, a car from one level to another on this than it would be to raise it vertically. It seems likely that the stones used for building the pyramids were moved on rollers pushed up earth ramps. A screw is really an inclined plane, but the slope is twisted round the shank of the screw. Run a piece of cotton along the thread from the top to tip and the length of the plane can be seen.

5 The work done by tools and machines can be roughly classified:

carrying
lifting
digging, scraping and scooping
cutting
boring and grinding
mixing, blending and stirring
hammering

levelling and smoothing
joining and stitching
drawing, writing and painting.

This list cannot cover every possible use of tools and leaves out those used for the textile crafts — spinning, weaving, knitting, dyeing — and such things as thatching, pottery making and many others, but it does give a basis on which to begin looking at tools and machines.

6 Weapons are tools, and these could be looked at with older children. It is possible to see many examples in museums all over the country. This study would start from the simple stone hand-axe and would include spears, bows and arrows, swords, axes, knives and guns. The stress could be on the use of materials — stone, wood, leather, bronze and iron.

PLANNING AND PREPARATION

1 Younger children can look at, and use, some of the simpler tools used for:

woodwork — hammer and nails, small saws and glues; they can also see planes, screw drivers, drills, and larger saws.
gardening — trowels and hand-forks, small spades, rakes, sieves; they can see how a wheelbarrow, a hoe and a lawnmower are used.
writing, drawing and painting — pencils, pens, crayons, brushes.
simple crafts — scissors, needles, brushes, rulers.
cooking — spoons, forks, hand-mixers, pastry cutters, rolling pins.

2 Older children can make collections of specialized tools, and can decide how these are used. They can write about each tool, describing its use. In some cases it will be necessary to collect pictures and not the actual tool.

Digging tools — trowels, spades, forks, shovels, heavy machinery for road-making.
Cutting tools — knives, axes, scissors, scythes, lawnmowers, saws and particular cutting tools like machetes and billhooks.
Drilling tools – carpenters' hand-drills, gimlets, brace and bit, oil-drilling equipment.

Tools for lifting — pulleys, levers, winches, fork-lift trucks, cranes.
Mixing and crushing tools — forks, spoons, hand-whisks, electric mixers, concrete mixers, pestles and mortars.
Tools and machines for moving things.
Power tools — using electricity, petrol motors etc.
Tools for particular crafts.

3 Using kits, such as Meccano, children can try to build cranes etc and can tell other children how these work.

4 Even the youngest children can cope with some sort of woodwork.

This can start with sticking together bits of pre-cut wood to make dolls house furniture, and can include the use of hammers and nails and small saws. Children can practise using a hammer by hitting nails into a log or thick piece of wood.

5 Using a plank of wood (at least 1m long) children can do some work on the use of slopes and ramps. The plank will need raised edges on the long sides. These can be made with strips of thick card glued or tacked to the edge, or wood quadrant can be nailed along the edge. If this is used as a slope (raised on one or two bricks) the children can find out if the incline of the slope makes any difference to the distance travelled by a toy car released at the top of the slope, and can find how much effort is needed to pull the car up the slope. If the slope is put on a table, a string can be attached to the car which can go up and over the end of the slope, and hang down. If weights (arbitrary or specific) are tied to the string, children can see how many are needed to pull up the car.

6 Wherever two surfaces rub together there is friction. Children can see this pushing a house brick across various surfaces — sandpaper, smooth plastic, paper, stone, fabric etc. They will see that the rougher the surface the greater the friction. Friction can be overcome in several ways — smooth surfaces, oil and grease and bearings. Experiments can be done to show this. The use of bearings can be shown by asking a child to stand on the lid of a syrup tin on one foot, and to try and twist round. The lid will not move, but put seven or eight marbles under the lid and ask him to try again. The movement will be easy because the marbles act as bearings.

WORKING AND RECORDING

The children can try the experiments mentioned above and can plan some of their own work. They will already know a great many tools and machines and can decide which areas they would like to study. This will vary from school to school and from district to district. Children living in a largely agricultural area will have a far greater knowledge of farm machinery than town children, but those living in towns may well, for example, have fathers working in the car industry. It may be possible to find parents with special skills or with capabilities in crafts which could be demonstrated at school and these will be invaluable for topics.

Any collections should be carefully labelled and, where possible, an example of the article made with the tools should be included, e.g. a finished cane basket and all the tools used to make it. If children use the tools themselves they can either write about their use, or explain this on a tape which can be used as part of the exhibition.

Lists can be made under headings:

tools found at home
tools found in the garage
tools found at school

road-working machinery
tools and machines in the kitchen
building tools
the carpenter's tools
tools used for specific crafts.

A game can be made using pictures of different tools stuck on cards. The children are asked to find out the names of the tools, and what they are used for.

Whatever work is done it should be recorded in some way so that other children can see it and there is a check on what the children have done. This can be done by:

making books about tools and their use
making scrap books
using tools and explaining orally how they were used
producing exhibitions
painting and drawing pictures on the use of tools and machines
making a commentary for a set of slides of machines or tools (commercially-produced slides can be used here)
making a frieze which is a historical time chart, e.g. 'The use of wheels through the ages'
making models of large machines — cranes, earth movers etc.

SUPPORT MATERIAL

Books for the children

Tools Gerard Bell (OUP)
Around the Home J. D. Bevington (Ginn) (Six small books)
Nails, Screws and Glue Starters Series (Macdonald Educational)
Tools and Weapons O. B. Gregory. (Wheaton)
Simple Machines T. S. Pine and J. Levine (Blackie)

Books for teacher reference

How to Start Using Tools Charles Graveney (Studio Vista)
Structures and Forces 1 and 2 Science 5/13 (Macdonald Educational)
General Science Book 3 Charles Windridge (Schofield & Sims)

Useful apparatus

Any tools available; hammers; nails; pulleys; wheeled toys; inclined plane; scissors; Meccano; glue; sandpaper; tin lids; marbles; pieces of wood; string.

16 SOMETHING ABOUT SOUND

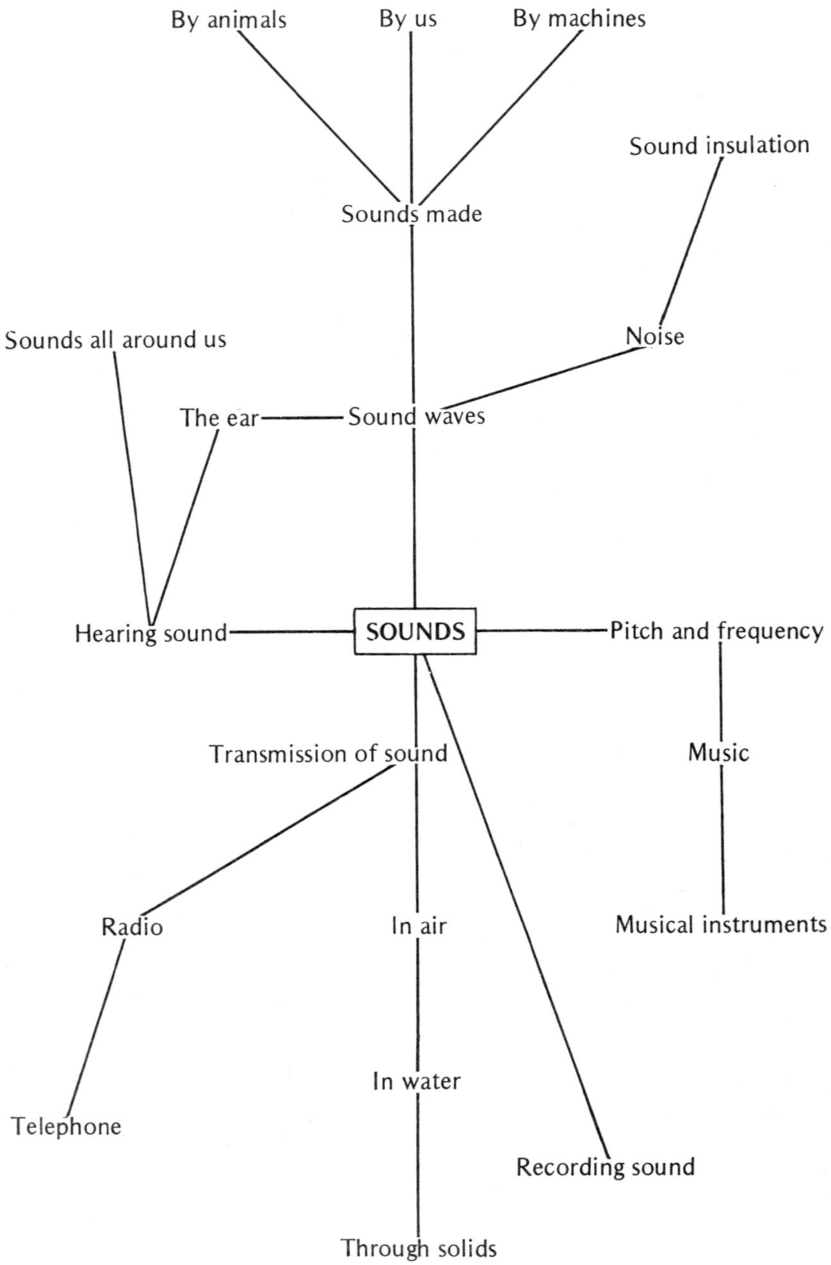

Children are aware of sounds all around them from the moment that they are born, but they do not necessarily listen to them. Many have become so used to the constant output from the radio or the television they they are more or less unaware of what is actually going on. There can be so much noise in a busy street that the individual sounds are virtually obliterated, and the habit of not really listening can be difficult to break.

If children can be made aware of the wide variation of different sounds, and if they can learn to distinguish one from another, they will be able to make a more rational choice as to what they want to listen to, and will be much more conscious of their own environment.

They need, also, to realize that sounds can be pleasant or unpleasant. To most people music, some speaking voices, such sounds as the swish of waves and the whisper of leaves and the dawn chorus of birds will be a definite pleasure. Other sounds will disturb and irritate, but it is only by listening that we can hear the sounds that please us and which can be a source of stimulation or relaxation.

GENERAL NOTES

1 Sound is produced by vibrations which cause waves to spread outwards from the source of the sound. Sound must have a medium through which to travel (it cannot travel through a vacuum) and this medium can be air, water or a solid.

2 Sound travels in air at a speed of approximately 1120 feet per second.

3 The more vibrations a second the higher will be the note produced; fewer vibrations give lower notes. This is called the pitch of a note. Loudness depends on the intensity of the sound, and loudness and pitch are not the same thing. A note can be loud and high pitched, or loud and low pitched etc.

4 If a sound bounces back it is called an echo; sound bounces off hard surfaces (rock and walls) better than it does off soft surfaces (curtains and carpets). This has to be taken into consideration in buildings where, for example, music is to be played or recordings made.

5 Regular vibrations give musical notes and pleasant sounds; irregular vibrations give noise. Noise is measured in decibels. The noise of two people talking quietly is about 20 decibels; a noise of 120 decibels is so loud that it can cause actual physical pain.

6 Sound is heard through the ears. Sounds cause the eardrums to vibrate, and these vibrations travel through tiny bones in the ear, called the ossicles, to the cochlea and finally to the nerves which carry the sound impressions to the brain. The ear is very sensitive and can normally pick up very soft sounds. It can also react to sounds of both high and low pitch, but very few people can hear the squeak of a bat because the frequency (the number of vibrations per second) is too great. A dog can hear notes above the range of human hearing.

7 The external ears of animals vary and children can look at these. In the mammals these are obvious, but children can also try to decide if birds, reptiles and fish can hear. The ears of the bird have no external lobes, but the ear openings, protected by feathers, lie behind the eyes. The frog has exposed eardrums at the side of the head. Along the sides of the fish is a line, called the lateral line, running from head to tail. This contains nerve cells sensitive to vibrations, but fish cannot hear in the way that the mammals can.

PLANNING AND PREPARATION

There are a number of experiments that young children can do to help them to understand more about the nature of sound.

1 They can listen to a prepared tape of sounds and try to say how these have been made. When making the tape, record sounds that are likely to be familiar to the children concerned, and only discuss four or five at one time, e.g. brushing teeth, tap running, a train, traffic noise, dog barking, clapping, hammering, lawnmower, bell ringing, crumpling paper, tearing cloth or paper, pouring a liquid, electric mixer.

2 If nails are hammered into a thick piece of wood so that they stick up about 3 cm, rubber bands can be stretched between them. The shorter the band the higher pitched the note given out if the band is plucked.

3 Various articles hung on a string and suspended from a suitable bar can be tapped with a stick or a pencil. The children can try to arrange these in order of pitch, e.g. bottle, empty tin, metal spoon, plastic spoon, matchbox, clay flower pot, large nail, cup.

4 A string telephone can be made with two empty baked bean cans (the tops removed cleanly, with a rotary opener), two matchsticks and a length (5–6 m) of thin, strong string. Make a hole in the bottom of each can and thread the string through these holes, so that the ends are inside the tins. Tie a matchstick to each end and pull the string tight. If a child holds one can over his ear, another can talk quietly into the other. The sound will travel along the taut string. Yoghurt cartons can be used instead of tins.

5 Two plastic funnels and a length of plastic tubing will make a toy stethoscope. Push the ends of the funnels into the plastic tubing, and if one funnel is held against a child's chest, and the other used for listening, the heartbeat can be heard. It is also possible to hear the faint tick of a watch if one funnel is placed over it.

6 Making simple musical instruments:

a Join two yoghurt pots with sticky tape after putting dried peas or rice in them. These make excellent shakers, and the sounds will vary according to whether they are shaken or rolled. Louder shakers can be made using tins with peas, rice or small stones in them.

b Use one of the large beer cans as a drum. This can be hit with small sticks or pencils. If both ends are removed, experiments can be made by stretching various materials over the ends and securing these with several strong rubber bands. This can be tried with strong paper, thin leather and plastic sheeting. As the materials need to be stretched very tightly this is not often successful with young children.

c Loosely thread metal milk bottle tops onto string and tie this to a short stick. This makes a pleasant rustling sound when shaken. Metal milk bottle tops can also be nailed loosely to a broom handle. When this is banged on the floor the bottle tops rattle.

d Two pieces of wood or broom handle can be banged together, and if sandpaper is glued to two pieces of wood these can be rubbed together.

e It is not easy to make pitched musical toys, but this can be tried with milk bottles. Eight bottles are needed; the first is filled with water and the last left empty. Those inbetween are graduated by varying the amount of water in each. These can be hit with a pencil or piece of dowel. With trial and error it is possible to graduate these so that a simple tune can be played. Suspended clay flower pots – of different sizes – will also produce different notes.

7 It is useful to collect together different musical instruments that the children can see and use:

instruments which are hit (percussion) — triangle, drum, tambourine, cymbals, blocks, xylophone
wind instruments — recorder, flute, clarinet
stringed instruments — guitar, violin, banjo (a piano is also a stringed instrument but the strings are hit with small hammers)

Any musical instruments which the children can see should be used.

WORKING AND RECORDING

The youngest children can start their work on sound by making sounds. They can see how many sounds they can make using nothing but their own bodies — clapping, rubbing, stamping, whistling, talking, singing, shouting, clicking their teeth. They can then find the sounds that can be made by hitting different things with a piece of stick. They can divide the sounds into loud sounds and soft sounds, and can make books of 'Nice Sounds' and 'Nasty Sounds'.

They can collect 'sound' words:

onomatopoeic words — buzz, bang, bump, thump, quack, squeak, splash, hiss, swish, tinkle, ding.
mouth words — talk, chatter, sigh, whisper, sing, shout, speak, call
noise words — crash, bang, thud, explosion, thunder
animal words — bark, squeak, mew, quack, twitter, crow, roar, growl, purr

music words — song, chant, tune, note, hymn
machine words — whir, clank, rasp.

Children can be asked to sit quite still, without speaking, for a minute and then to say all the sounds they heard. They can go on a 'sound' walk and can list all the sounds they hear. They can make a frieze of animal pictures and add a label giving the sound made by each of these.

Older infants can do the various experiments suggested and can explain how they did these, and what they found out.

Simple musical instruments can be made and used. If these are accompanied by a piano or a recorder the percussion type can be used to play a simple tune. This can be recorded and played back to the children. Alternatively the instruments can be used as sound effects e.g. making sea noises, sound of wind, things falling, jungle noises, sound of walking or running, clock ticking, water runnning. The children can either make up a story between them, or can use a well-known story and use their instruments to go with this. Remember that the voice is a useful instrument, too.

Children can see and use real musical instruments. They can classify these in various ways, and can explain how the sounds are made. They can listen to records of music and see if they can pick out any instruments, and they can find out what sort of music different people like.

Children can devise their own experiments to solve problems set for them. These can be put onto cards and the children can record their answers in a 'Sounds Book'. Some examples of 'problems' are given below:

1	From how far away can we hear sounds? Using the clock, make up an experiment to find out how far the sound of the ticking travels.

2	Will sounds travel through wood? Can you make up some experiments to find this out?

3	Is it possible to muffle sounds? Use the alarm clock and wind it up so that the alarm will go off. See if you can cover, or wrap up, the clock so that the alarm cannot be heard.

Different books can be made on aspects of sound work; and exhibitions could be put together to show, for example:

Nice and nasty sounds — using pictures

Musical instruments
Sound experiments
How sound travels
Musical toys
How we hear
Animal sounds
Ears

SUPPORT MATERIAL

Books for the children

Sounds and Music First Library Series (Macdonald Educational)
Things to Hear Henry Pluckrose (Franklin Watts)
Sound Things Romola Showell (Ward Lock Educational)
Sounds Allan P. Sanday (Ladybird Books)
Sound Denis Wrigley (Lutterworth Press)
Sounds and Music R. H. C. Fice and M. Simkiss (E. J. Arnold)

Books for teacher reference

Early Experiences Science 5/13 (Macdonald Educational)
General Science Book 4 Charles Windridge (Schofield & Sims)
The Observer's Book of Music Freda Dinn (Frederick Warne)
Introduction to Biology (for information on ears and hearing) D. G. Mackean (John Murray).

Useful apparatus

Broom handles; dowel; rubber bands; blocks of wood; nails; hammer; collection of tins and plastic pots; dried peas; rice; alarm clock; string; spoons; pictures of animals; plastic funnels; plastic tubing; clean milk bottles; toys that make sounds (rattle, humming top, toy piano, clicking toys, whistles etc); clay flower pots; tape recorder; and musical instruments.

Record or tape of the sounds of musical instruments.

17 WALLS

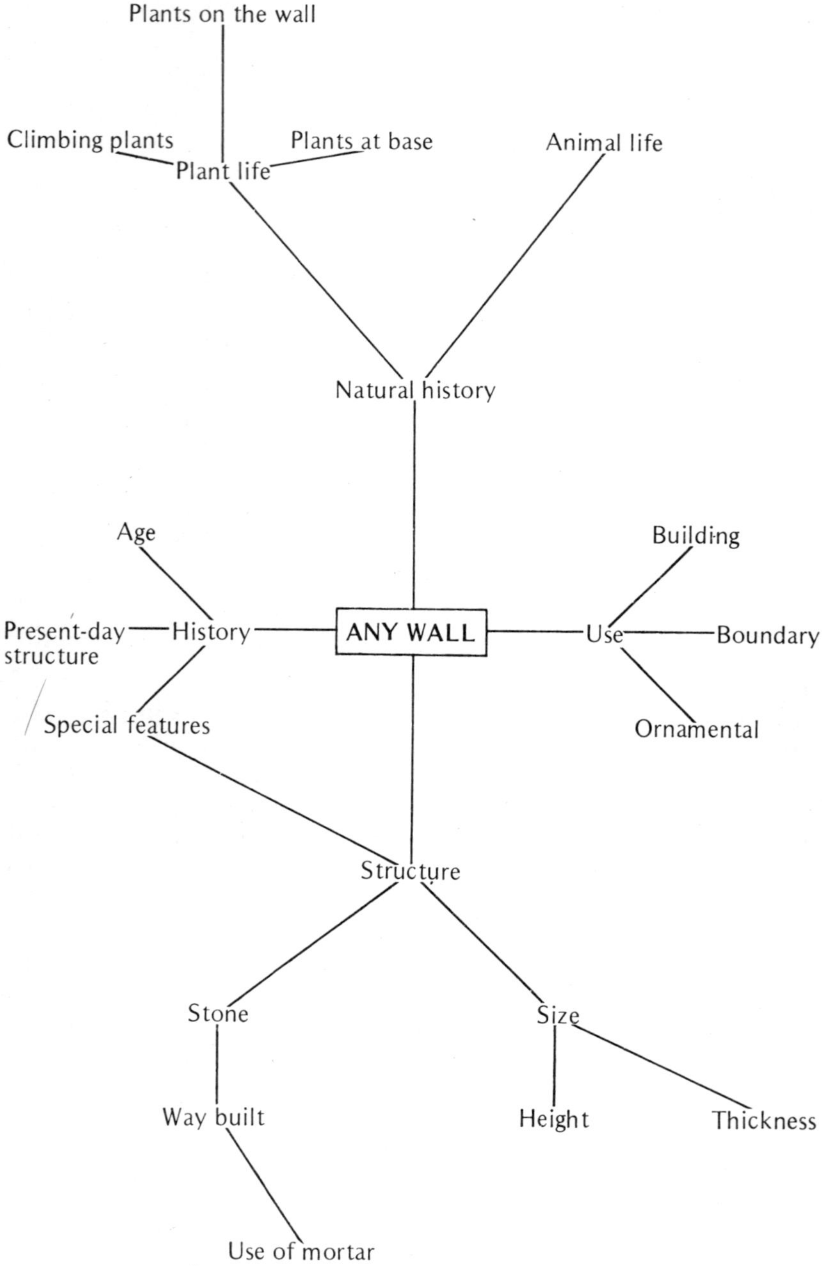

Plants on the wall
Climbing plants
Plants at base
Plant life
Animal life
Natural history
Age
Building
Present-day structure
History
ANY WALL
Use
Boundary
Special features
Ornamental
Structure
Stone
Size
Way built
Height
Thickness
Use of mortar

Wherever the school is situated, and whatever the type of environment, there are always walls to be found. They may be the very old walls of a Norman castle or they may be found on a newly-built housing estate, but the way they are built, their purposes, their history and any living organisms connected with them will provide the basis for an investigation by children. Because of the proximity of walls of all types they make a suitable study for any class at any time of the year. They are a useful link between several study areas — science (natural history, structure, type of stone used), history (age, style, purpose), mathematics (size, shape, strength, tessellation). Stories about walls can be introduced, starting with the well-known one about Humpty Dumpty!

A look at the walls of the school is a good starting point. How old is the building? How are the walls built? Are they made of brick, stone or other materials? If they are made of bricks or stones are these arranged in any particular pattern? Is there any sign of weathering? Is there any plant growth on the walls?

Old walls are probably the most interesting, but because any walls are so common they can be used to show children that there is always something interesting to be found if only they will look around them and think about what they see.

GENERAL NOTES

1 Some walls are built of natural stone. These may be coursed (laid in regular layers), uncoursed (built of irregular blocks), pointed with mortar or cement, or they may have small pebbles between the larger stones. Natural stone tends to be used in the districts where the stones are found, e.g. Cotswold limestone, Cornish slate. Stone has been used for building since ancient times. It was first used in the parts of the country where stone was easily available — Wiltshire and Yorkshire, for example.

2 Natural stone walls were also built as field boundaries — usually stone and earth walls, slate walls or dry stone walls. Particular features of boundary walls can be looked for — stiles, gates, slabs set as steps for climbing over the wall, hogg holes etc. (A hogg hole is a small hole in a wall to allow a small sheep [a hoog or hogget] to get through, but not a large sheep or cow. They are mostly found in walls in North of England and Scotland where the word hogg is used.) Dry stone walls are built without mortar and are made up of rocks and stones fitted together to make very strong and stable structures. These walls are common in the north and west, but rare in the south and, unfortunately, many are disappearing as they are torn down to enlarge fields. Most dry stone walls are wider at the base, and the stones are chosen and placed with care so that there are very few gaps. If children live in a rocky area they could try building a small wall themselves.

3 The use of evenly-sized bricks for wall building means that work can be carried out more quickly. There are different ways of laying

A hogg hole built into a stone wall

Common brick bonds

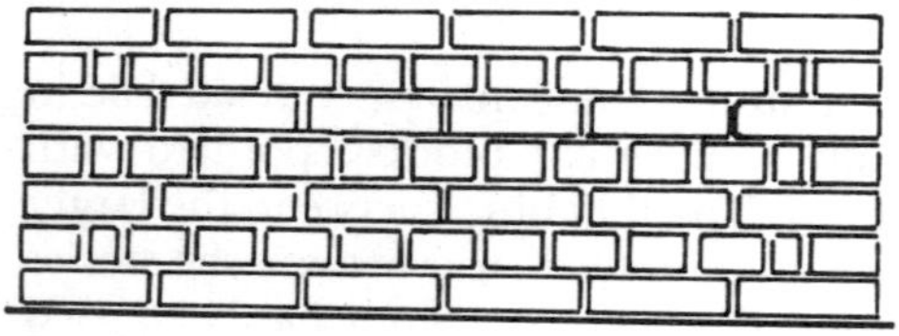

English bond (the strongest)

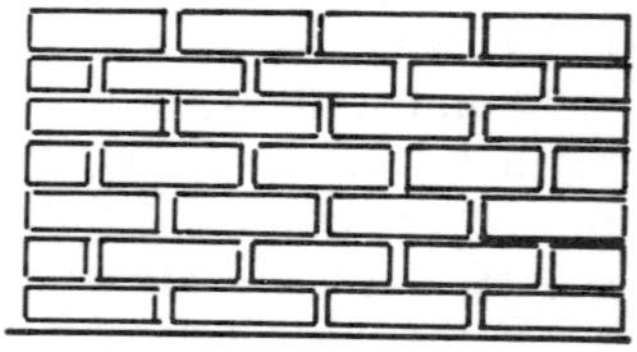

Stretcher bond

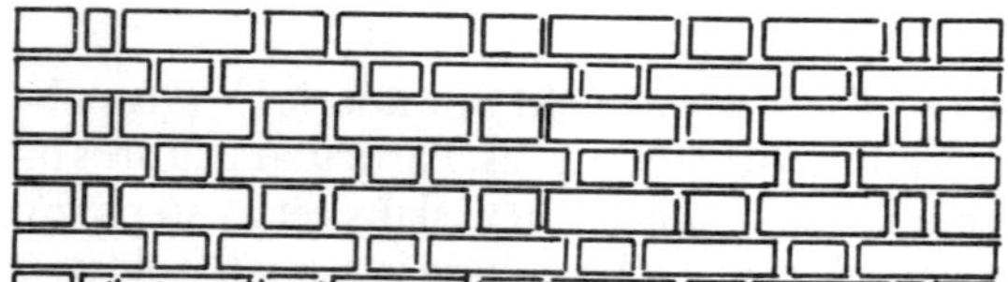

Flemish bond

Uncoursed squared rubble – 'cocks and hens' stone coping

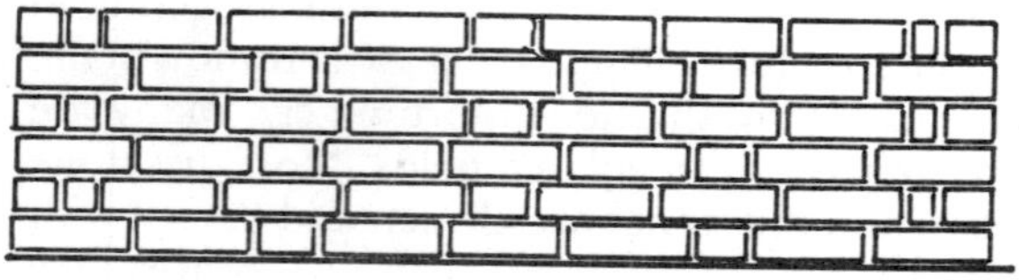

Sussex bond

bricks. It is possible to see these different patterns, or bonds, in any brick-built wall. The commonest are the English bond, the Flemish bond and heading bond.

An uncommon way of using bricks is to lay them in a herring-bone pattern. This can sometimes be seen in very old walls; one example can be seen at Tamworth Castle in Staffordshire. Bricks are bound together with mortar or cement, and it is valuable if the children can see a professional bricklayer at work.

4 Examples of walls in towns:

a old and new walls on buildings of all sorts. These can be stone, brick, prefabricated concrete blocks etc.
b church walls
c remains of town walls; castles
d railway bridges and retaining walls
e garden and park walls
f factory buildings.

5 Examples of walls in the country:

a houses — old and new
b castles and fortifications
c churches
d dams
e field boundaries
f gardens
g specific historical walls and buildings — e.g. Hadrian's Wall.

6 Wall features:

a date and name stones
b sundials
c straighteners
d buttresses
e arches, doors and gateways
f niches, statues, carvings and ornamentation
g capping stones.

7 Natural history of walls:

a plants growing on the wall; roots between the stones, in crevices etc, e.g. Ivy-leaved Toadflax, Stonecrop, Mosses, Lichens, Ferns.
b plants climbing the wall but with their roots in the ground, e.g. Ivy.
c plants growing at the base of a wall, e.g. Grasses, Dock, Nettles, Dandelion, Vetch, Bramble.
d animals found on the wall and among the stones, e.g. Snails, Spiders, Woodlice, Ants, Earwigs.
e animals seen on and near walls, e.g. Field Mice, birds (Sparrows, Starlings, Robins, Wagtails, Pigeons). Some of the Owls will nest on ledges of ruined buildings.

Identifying and classifying Ferns, Mosses and Lichens is too difficult for young children, but they can find out the names of other plants from suitable books (and with help).

PLANNING AND PREPARATION

1 Look at walls in the area of the school or in places that the children can visit. Decide what sort of work young children could do.

Have the walls any historical significance?
Are the walls part of buildings?
Are they decorative or just functional?
Are the walls boundaries of some sort?
Of what material are they built?
Have they any interesting features?
Are there any plants growing on or alongside them?
Are there any animals connected with the walls?

2 Plan a visit to a site where children can look at a wall. Take photographs of it with the children and let them make rubbings. Use thin, strong paper and thick black wax crayons. Brick walls make extremely good rubbings, and the brick bonds show up well. Collect samples of any plants growing in or on the wall. Teach the children to ask you first about picking plants, and show them which they can take back to the classroom. Plants can be pressed if the children want to keep examples of what they have found. Put each plant between two layers of blotting paper, and then between several layers of newspaper. Put them under a very heavy weight (e.g. a cupboard or bookshelf) or into a press. They need to be left for several weeks, so pressing will not give an instant result. Before pressing the plants could be named, and the children could draw them.

3 Collect samples of stone, rock and brick for the children to see. They can scratch them with a large nail to test for hardness, and can put them into water to see if they are porous. Using house bricks, the children can try to build a wall. If possible build this with a purpose in mind (e.g. walling off a small corner of the playground to make a plant trough). Packs of ready mixed sand and cement can be bought, but it is cheaper to mix your own.

4 Bricks for making models can be made from clay using matchbox trays for moulds. When the clay is dry the bricks can be used for building. Different ways of placing the bricks can be tried out.

5 Wall straighteners can be seen on many old walls. These are usually seen as an iron-cross bar or an H shape. Basically a strong metal pin is placed through the wall. One end is attached to the outside bar, and on the inside another bar is screwed onto the pin. Before tightening the metal is heated so that it expands. It is then screwed up tightly. As the pin cools the metal contracts and the pull straightens the wall. A buttress is used to support a high wall and can be seen on many old

buildings; look at churches and castles.

6 To make mortar use sand and cement in the proportion of three parts sand to one of cement, mixed with water. Experiments could be done using different proportions, and if each mix is made into a small brick and left to dry children can test for strength by trying to break them, dropping them etc.

7 Devise a project sheet for older infants which can be duplicated and which they can fill in to record wall features, e.g

Walls
Where is the wall? . . . .
How old is it?. . . . .
What is it? Part of a building . . . .
Boundary wall. . . . .
What is it made of? . . . .
Tick any of these seen on the wall:
Moss . . . . Lichen . . . . Ferns . . . . Ivy . . . . . .
Grass. . . . . Other plants . . . .
Have you found any animals? . . . .
What? . . . .

WORKING AND RECORDING

Younger children can go and look at a wall, they can make rubbings and can collect plant specimens. Back in the classroom the wall can be drawn as an outline on a large sheet of paper and the children can add features seen — a name plaque, Ivy growing on it (this can be made as separate leaves, and then these can be stuck on), Snails, Dandelions at the base, Sparrows seen on the top etc.

Pictures can be collected from magazines (and all teachers should keep a resource box of pictures from magazines, colour supplements, brochures etc; these always come in useful for topic work) showing walls and buildings. These could be made into a scrap book.

Children can experiment with building using real or model bricks, stones, slate or anything available. They can attempt a dry stone wall, and can use mortar to hold bricks together. Later they can explain how they did this work either in writing or on tape. They can also test the strength of mortar mixes.

Using a project sheet they can make a detailed study of a particular wall. The sheet will give them some basic information and from this they can build up a detailed study. The children could work in groups on:

a History of the wall (and even a new wall has a 'history'). When was it built? Why? Is it part of a new housing estate or factory?
b Structure of the wall — stone used, pattern of building, use of mortar or mud to hold it together, height, thickness.
c Details of the wall — ornamentation, carving, gates, doorways,

holes, stiles, name plates, road signs etc.

d Natural history — plants on it, plants under it, animals associated with it.

e Wear and weathering — is it damaged or worn? Is there any particular reason for this? Is it dirty (smoke grime in towns, particularly)? Has any part of it fallen? Have any parts apparently been added later?

It may be possible for children to make a collection of bricks, particularly if they know anyone associated with demolition. These will vary in size, colour and texture; some will have holes or hollows in them; some will have names or initials. The children can also find out if they all weigh the same.

They can do a topic simply on the natural history of walls and can try and find out how plants can grow without having their roots in the ground. They can also find out how Ivy grows up walls, how plant seeds could have got to the top of high walls, whether there are different types of Mosses and what Lichens look like (a binocular microscope would be useful here). They could mount a display of wall plants using actual examples, drawings and paintings and books showing pictures of the specimens.

The oldest infants could produce a topic book dealing with particular walls such as Hadrian's wall, the Great Wall of China, the old town walls of their own town, sea walls, dams etc.

SUPPORT MATERIAL

Books for the children

Look at Walls Starters Series (Macdonald Educational)
Weeds Mollie Clarke (Hart-Davis)
Science from the Beginning Book 1 B. L. Hampson and K. C. Evans (Oliver and Boyd)

Books for teacher reference

Looking Around in Town and Country Philip Sauvain (Franklin Watts)
Structures and Forces Science 5/13 (Macdonald Educational)
Junior Science Source Book J. W. Bainbridge, R. W. Stockdale and E. R. Wastnedge (Collins)
Any simple flora.

Useful apparatus

Hand-lenses; binocular microscrope; matchboxes; cement; sand; clay; plant press (or two thick sheets of plywood 30cm x 30cm and two G-clamps); blotting paper; camera; wax crayons; house bricks; tape recorder.

18 HEDGEROWS

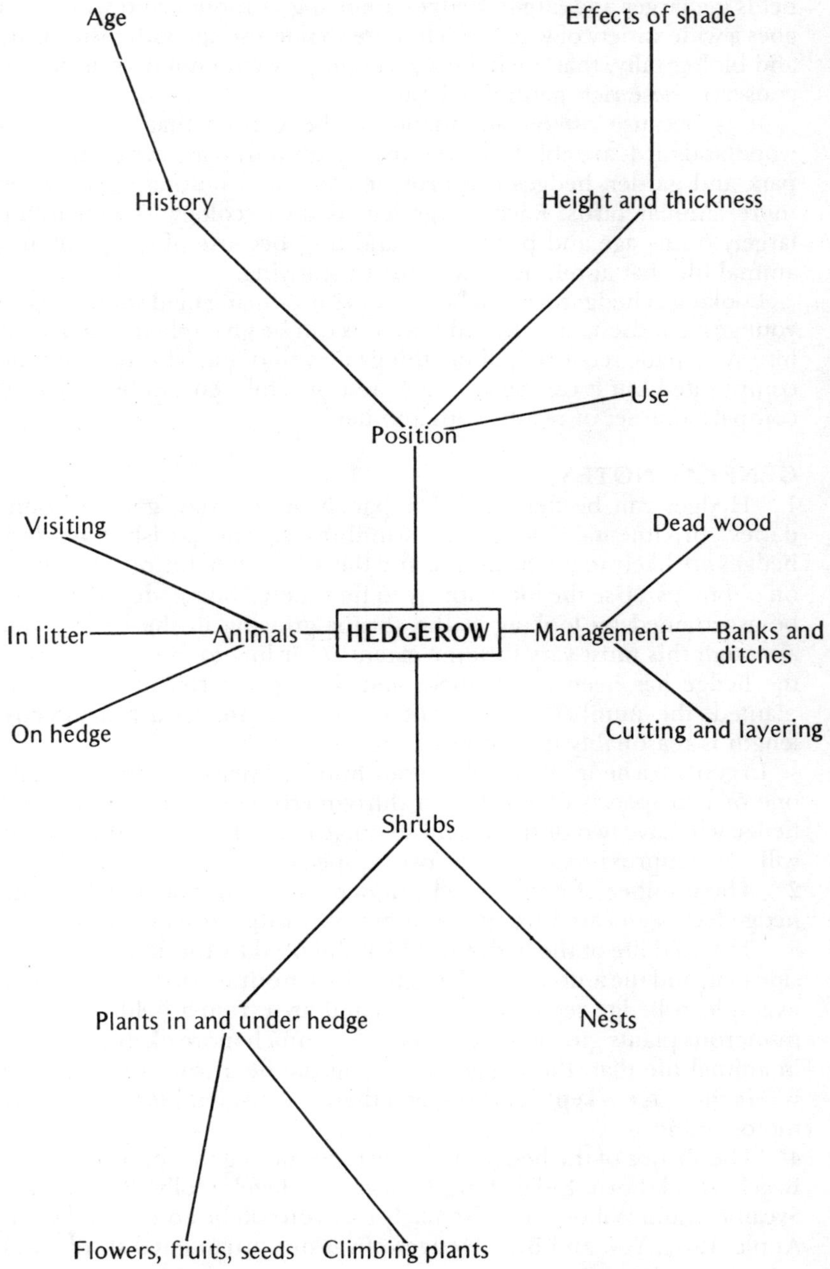

If you stand on high ground and look around at the countryside you can see the patchwork of fields. Most fields will be separated by hedges which are still so plentiful that they form valuable nature reserves, but as fields get larger and larger, hedges are being uprooted, and with them goes a wide variety of wild life. They are so interesting, both historically and biologically, that it will be a great pity if we do not do our best to conserve these rich natural habitats.

It is because of the abundance of hedgerows that our natural woodland birds are able to survive in agricultural areas, and even newer park and garden hedges can provide cover and nesting sites for the more familiar birds. Each hedge has its own ecology — depending largely on its age and position — and this, because of the plant and animal life that abounds, is well worth studying.

Looking at hedgerows can be a way of introducing field studies to the youngest children, and the older infants can be given their first insight into systematic recording of the things they find out. This need not be complicated but it can be accurate, and the children can be taught to compare one set of results with another.

GENERAL NOTES

1 Hedges can be field, road or parish boundaries, garden boundaries, ornamental features or windbreaks. The parish boundary hedges are likely to be the oldest, and these can often be found marked on old maps. (Use the local library to find these.) Some idea of age can be ascertained by looking at the shrubs growing in the hedge, and although this must vary to some extent according to the way in which the hedge has been maintained, and the type of soil in which it is planted, the number of different shrubs growing in a thirty-metre length is reasonably indicative of age.

In general a hedge that is about one hundred years old will have only one or two species of shrub in a thirty-metre length; a 200 year old hedge will have two or three, and so on. A hedge that is 1000 years old will have approximately ten or twelve species.

2 The number of nests found will depend on the way in which the hedge has been cared for, the number of shrubs present and the site.

3 The wild life of the hedge will be influenced by the areas on either side of it, and the amount of plant growth in the immediate vicinity. For example, a hedge separating a woodland area from a field, and with numerous plants growing underneath it, is much more likely to be rich in animal life than the hedge separating the field from the roadside where the verge is kept cut short, and there is considerable pollution by motor traffic.

4 The shrubs of the hedge are likely to be among the following: Ash, Beech, Blackthorn, Elder, Elm, Hawthorn, Hazel, Holly, Privet, Oak, Sycamore and Willow. It is also likely that you will be able to find Crab Apple, Rose, Yew and Box. Hedges of various ornamental shrubs will

be found in parks and gardens.

5 Plants growing under and in the hedge will vary according to districts but children will be able to find grasses, Bramble, Hogweed, Bryony, Ivy, Campion, Dandelion, Vetch, Cleavers, Burdock, Dock etc. Ferns may be growing in some hedges, and plants such as Cuckoo Pint and Primrose which are less common.

6 Animal life can include caterpillars of various Butterflies and Moths, Beetles, Spiders, Snails, Harvestmen, Bees, Frogs and Toads. Other visitors may be Field Mice, Voles, Hedgehogs, Grasshoppers, Rabbits, Lizards and birds nesting in the hedge or feeding on the plant seeds and insects.

PLANNING AND PREPARATION

1 If children are going to study a section of hedgerow it is worth visiting it first so that you know what can be found and what preparations you will need to make for collecting specimens. Basically thirty metres of hedge makes a reasonable study, but with the younger children it would probably be better to look well at a ten-metre section. Choose the most interesting area for them — where there is plentiful plant growth, and a number of different species. See if there is any litter (in this case, the plant debris found under hedges and trees) which is likely to house small animals such as woodlice, centipedes etc.

2 Prepare children for a visit, and see that they know some of the countryside rules. Make certain that they know that they must never touch nests (particularly if the visit is to be in spring) or eggs, that they do not damage the hedge in any way, and that they only collect plant and animal specimens with your permission. Any rocks or logs moved should be put back carefully. These may be the mini-habitats of many small animals.

3 Older children can be provided with a survey sheet, and this could be used to compare one stretch of hedge with another. It will also help to teach them how to identify plants.

Hedges	**Project Sheet**
Name. . . . . (of child)	Date of visit . . . .
Tick type of hedge: (it may be more than one of these)	Field boundary. . . . .
	Roadside . . . .
	Parish boundary. . . . .
	Garden. . . . .
	Ornamental . . . .

Is the hedge uncut? . . . .

Has it been cut lately? . . . .

It is layered? . . . .

Hedge shrubs: (tick those you have found)

Ash . . .	Beech	Blackthorn . . .
Elder	Elm	Hawthorn . . . .
Hazel	Holly	Oak . . . .
Privet	Willow	Sycamore . . . .

Other shrubs . . . .

Plants growing under the hedge:

Plants climbing in the hedge:

Plants growing near the hedge:

Are there any nests? . . .   How many? . . .

Birds seen:

Insects found:

Other animals found or seen:

Anything else interesting:

Obviously children will need help in identifying plants, and if these are not known, specimens could be taken back to school for later identification.

4 Children living in a country area may be able to see how a hedge is cut and layered. The need for thick hedges, if they are to keep animals from straying, will be fairly obvious, and they can also discuss other uses of hedges, e.g. to show the boundary between peoples' land; to act as a windbreak, to provide shelter for farm animals.

5 If a hedge can be visited at different seasons the children can build up a profile of the hedge over the year. Town children are not always going to have the opportunity of visiting an interesting hedgerow, but they could make a study of hedges in general, and often they can be found in the most unlikely areas. A row of very old Hawthorns growing

in the middle of a town park, or on an open space, almost always indicates that a hedge has once been present, and the Hawthorns were probably on farm land. Garden and park hedges are often 'pure' hedges, i.e. they have only one predominant shrub. Children can use these to find out if some shrubs support more wild life than others.

6 Children will need some collecting equipment for a hedgerow visit. Small plastic bags can be used for leaves, flowers, seeds, grasses and fungi. Larger plastic bags will be needed for such things as a disused nest, stones, bark etc. Small pots with perforated lids can be used for Woodlice, Ladybirds and caterpillars etc. If the children find a caterpillar make sure that they know which plant it was feeding on. If you want to keep caterpillars in the classroom they will need supplies of their particular food plant.

WORKING AND RECORDING

Having found a suitable hedgerow for the children to visit the work can be planned according to the age of the children involved. The youngest children can look at the hedge, see the plants growing in it and around it, and make collections of grasses, leaves and flowers. They can watch any small animals found and can draw pictures of these. Beetles, such as Ladybirds, can have their shape cut out of red card, and the children can stick the spots on them.

A long outline of the hedge can be cut out of frieze paper and the children can build this up with cut-out shapes to show the plants found there. To this can be added birds, butterflies, beetles, caterpillars or anything else that the children have seen.

Older children can make more specific collections of specimens and pictures:

plants growing in the hedge
plants growing at the base
climbing plants
grasses growing at the base
animals found
leaf collections
fruits and seeds (if the work is done in the autumn).

The oldest infants can study a particular length of hedge and different groups (possibly ability groups) can make detailed surveys of differing areas of work. Some can fill in survey sheets, planned beforehand. The children themselves can decide on what should be put into these surveys and once this has been decided the sheets can be duplicated.

Others can try to decide on the age of the hedge (if this is not already known). First they will need to discuss the ways of working out the approximate age and the use of the hedge being studied. They will need some help with identification and some good pictures of the possible shrubs likely to be found. If the hedge is, say, a field boundary or round a garden they may be able to talk to the owner and find out something about it.

Another group can look to see how the hedge has been made. Is it layered? Has any of it been planted or replanted recently? What shrubs have been used to do this? Is it made of ornamental shrubs? Has it been cut recently? How was it cut? If it has a roadside verge on one side has the verge been cut? Has this cutting disturbed the plant and animal life at all? Has the stretch of hedge any gates or stiles? Does the hedge grow on a bank? Is there a ditch on either side?

A fourth group could study unusual features. They could, for example, take apart an old nest (make sure that the children understand that only old nests can be removed, and then only with your permission) and find out its constituents. They can weigh the nest and then list all the materials found in it (sticks, leaves, mud, feathers, sheep's wool etc).

Other examples are:

a Sheep's wool found on the hedge. This could be gathered, and then spun on hand spindles.

b Rubbish found in the hedge. This could be listed, and the children could discuss the dangers, to animals, of polythene bags, glass bottles and tins. They can include both farm and wild animals.

c Brambles near and twined into the hedge will produce Blackberries in the autumn. These could be picked and made into jam. Other fruits and seeds could be looked at and other edible ones found. It is also important to discuss inedible and poisonous plants at the same time.

d Part of the boundary may have remains of walls, and these can be looked at with the hedge.

e If there is a ditch this can be looked at to see if it contains any animal life.

One stretch of hedge can be compared with another, and the children could write up an account of the differences found. They could use photographs to illustrate structure, size and diversity of plant life.

If a hedge can be visited at different seasons an overall portrait can be built up, and an exhibition could be mounted to show what they have found. Photographs will be particularly useful for this, and tape-recorded commentaries describing the hedge at different times of the year will make a useful record. Slides, with a taped commentary made by the children, will remind them of what they have seen, and the programme made could be shown to other children.

With a written account and an exhibition, individual studies can be included. These can be done by one or two children who show a particular interest in any one aspect, e.g.

a collage of grasses found
leaf rubbings
fruits and seeds that are moved by the wind
fruits and seeds that can be eaten by animals
signs of animal life (leaves eaten by caterpillars; cuckoo spit; animal bones; Snail shells; insect remains; Owl pellets; Rabbit droppings; Sheep's wool).

All the written and pictorial work can be collected together into a class book, and this can include work from every child. This work can show children the various ways in which a systematic study can be made, and it should be undertaken with the idea of producing scientific, even if very simple, observations of what has been seen.

SUPPORT MATERIAL

Books for the children

Exploring the Hedgerow Leslie Jackson (Evans)
Plants and How They Grow F. E. Newing and R. Boxwood (Ladybird Books)
The Tree and Its World Romola Showell (Ladybird Books)
Let's Look at Insects Deborah Manley (Ward Lock)

Books for teacher reference

Wild Flowers of Verges and Waste Land Jean Imrie (A. and C. Black)
Ecology of Woodlands Alfred Leutscher (Franklin Watts)
The Oxford Book of Invertebrates D. Nichols and John Cooke (OUP)
A Field Guide to Mushrooms and Toadstools Morten Lange and F. Bayard Hora (Collins)
A Field Guide to the Trees of Britain and Northern Europe Alan Mitchell (Collins)
School Projects in Natural History: Nature Conservation The Devon Trust for Nature Conservation (Heinemann)
Any simple flora.

Useful apparatus

Camera; hand-lenses; plastic bags; lidded jars and pots; wax crayons; boxes for collections; tape recorder; Plasticine; slide projector; tape measures; string; glue; adhesive tape.

19 TOWN BIOLOGY

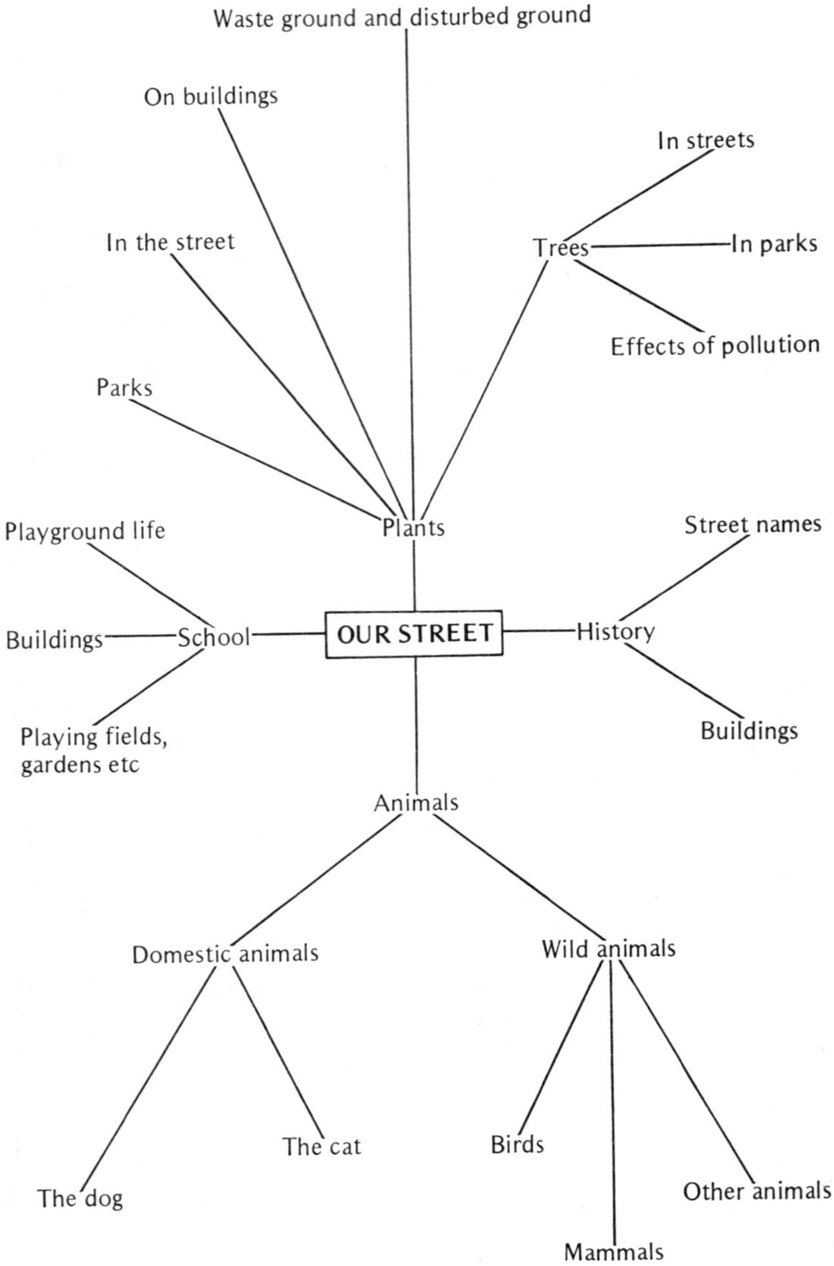

The natural history of the countryside is an obvious subject for study, but looking at the ecology of town wildlife can be both practical and rewarding. The word 'ecology' comes from two Greek words — *logos* meaning the study of, and *oikos* meaning homes — so it is the study of plant and animal life in their own environment.

This environment may be an unlikely industrial town or city, but many plants and animals are able to live there successfully and have established themselves so well that they have become a part of the town's profile. Sometimes traces of old habitats can be found — park land that is the remaining part of a natural forest, remnants of old hedges, vestigial river shores, old trees, old gardens — but other, newer habitats gradually build up in the area, and it is often possible to trace original agricultural or village life from street names. Look at the names of some of the older streets in the centre of any city and such names as Orchard Street, Mill Lane, Green Lane, Far Fold and Woodland Croft will be found.

Buildings resemble, in some ways, the rocks of cliffs and mountains, and Mosses will establish themselves on buildings, as on these, in time. Mosses hold water and tend to collect debris which gradually forms a growing base for such plants as Grasses, Ragwort and Dandelion. Birds which, in their original natural state, roost on rocks will nest and roost on the ledges of buildings (e.g. Starling, Pigeon, Wagtail).

Gardens, sports grounds and parks provide imitations of woodland and pasture land, and trees can also be found in streets. There may be reservoirs and canals providing aquatic habitats, and schools may have grounds with plants growing in them. These plants will shelter a host of small animals.

Any study based on the biology of the town environment — whether it is in the centre of a factory area or in a more open suburb — should start with the area immediately round the school. However barren this may appear to be there is always something to study and children, encouraged to look, may when they are older realize that we need not only to conserve the best of what exists but to add to the environment by clearing polluted areas, planting trees and preserving historically interesting buildings.

PLANNING AND PREPARATION

1 Go and look at the area round the school so that walks and visits can be planned for the children.

a *The school* Walls may have Mosses and Lichens on them (though Lichens do not grow well in a polluted atmosphere). Dandelions, Groundsel etc may be growing at the base and in cracks. There may be mown grass and the number of weeds in this can be looked at. If there is a playing field the edges may not be mown as closely and other weeds may be found. There may be planted borders of shrubs, bulbs etc, and planted trees. There may be regular bird visitors (Sparrows are often seen picking up pieces of biscuit and crisps dropped by children in playgrounds). Other bird visitors can be encouraged by regular feeding on a bird table.

b *Local parks and gardens* Parks vary from open spaces with a few outdoor toys to well planted and grassed areas with ponds and streams. Gardens may well be the front gardens of houses in nearby roads, but children can still see the hedges, flowers, shrubs and trees in these.

c *Churchyards and open spaces in city centres*

d *Old buildings* Look up as well as down. There may be plants growing on the roofs or in the guttering.

e *Canals, reservoirs and railway lines* Whilst none of these is an ideal site for very young children, there may be some parts which can be looked at safely. If this is possible the children can see the number of plants growing, and can see if there are any water birds on the canals and reservoirs.

f *Waste land* Areas of waste land are almost mini nature-reserves, and the variety of plant and animal life to be found can be quite surprising. It will depend, largely, on how long the area has lain waste as to which plants have established themselves.

g *The streets* Some weeds may be found growing almost anywhere. There are very few areas completely devoid of plant life, but weeds are looked on as things to be destroyed, and so only those which can germinate and flower in a short time are likely to be found in places where they will be disturbed by weedkillers, uprooting, traffic, rebuilding etc. Some of the weeds most likely to be found are Plantain, Dandelion, Groundsel, Rosebay Willow Herb (called Fire Weed in the USA because it is usually the first plant to grow after a fire), Shepherd's Purse, Meadow Grass, Rye Grass and Charlock.

2 Many species of birds are established in towns, and the Sparrows, Pigeons and Starlings are the most familiar. Most of the Pigeons seen are feral domestic Pigeons which are descendants of the wild Rock Dove, but Wood Pigeons are also found. Starlings are very common. During the day they tend to fly out of the town centres into fields or gardens to search for food, but come back to roost at night. The noise they make as they arrive in the evening can be considerable, and their droppings seriously deface many public buildings. Many ways have been tried to stop them roosting — bird scarers and sticky substances on ledges — but they never seem to stay away for long!

The commonest bird is the House Sparrow, seen wherever there is human habitation. These birds seem able to adapt themselves to almost any environment and can be attracted into any school playground by a regular supply of food.

Other birds seen feeding in towns include Magpies, Crows and Gulls — particularly around rubbish tips, and Tits and Greenfinches can be

attracted into city centres with strings of nuts and coconut.
3 The mammals of towns can be wild or domestic. Rats and Mice are not welcome visitors in most buildings, and Mice seem able to survive in any surroundings — probably because they will eat almost anything. As they tend to move around at night children are not likely to see them very often, and the same applies to Rats. They should, however, be mentioned when talking about town animals, and the children can see pictures or slides of them. Other animals found in towns, but which the children are not likely to see easily, are the Fox (becoming more and more common in urban areas), the Grey Squirrel, the Hedgehog and the Bat. The domestic animals are much more familiar — the Dog and the Cat — and these should not be ignored. They are a part of the town's natural history and are also easily available for children to study.
4 Other animals: Children can look for smaller animals in cracks in walls, under stones, on waste ground, in churchyards, in bicycle sheds, round the school playing field, in the park and on street trees. These will include Woodlice, Earwigs, Spiders (House and Garden Spiders), Beetles – particularly the Violet Ground Beetle – the Cockroach, Ants, Houseflies, Wasps, and some of the Butterflies and Moths.
5 Soil will be disturbed anywhere the ground is being cleared, where demolition is being carried out or where ground is being dug up for various reasons. If the ground is left without further disturbance for some time the plant life will re-establish itself. The first plants to grow will be the annuals, particularly those with seeds dispersed by the wind. These include Willow Herb, Groundsel, Ragwort, Meadow Grass, Shepherd's Purse and Chickweed. Gradually other plants will appear — Dandelion, Dock, Plantain, Mayweed, Thistles, other Grasses.
6 Trees can be found in parks, gardens, school grounds, churchyards and along walks and streets. The Plane is a common town tree. It has managed to survive dirty and smoky conditions because its bark continuously peels off getting rid of the accumulated dirt and its leaves tend to repel dust and grime. Lime and Sycamore also grow well in a town, and it is common to find Beech, Birch, Laburnum, Maple and Hawthorn. Planted trees need to be able to tolerate the conditions of town life with its traffic and air pollution, and evergreens are not really suitable. As they keep their leaves accumulations of dirt build up on them to such an extent that the trees are unable to breathe or absorb light energy.

WORKING AND RECORDING

The youngest children can start by looking at their own schools. They can see how many different plants — including trees — they can find and can make large wall pictures showing, for example, the school building and the plants associated with it. If the plant pictures are made separately they can be cut out and stuck onto the picture. If insects and birds have also been found, these can be added to the picture.

The plants can be grouped in some way:

plants growing on or near the wall
plants growing in the borders
plants growing round the playground
plants growing along the fence.

A plan can be made of the adjacent streets and the position of any trees can be shown. These can be named, and identification cards can be made. Each card should have the name of the tree, a bark rubbing, a pressed leaf or a leaf rubbing, and an outline picture of the tree. At this stage enthusiasm is far more important than absolute accuracy, and the children should be encouraged to look and then to produce the best pictures they can.

Take the children on a street walk and get them to note all the plants that they see, and teach them to look upwards — many Mosses and plants grow above eye level. They may find unusual plants or garden plants that have established themselves in strange places, and if there is any waste ground it is worth collecting plant specimens so that these can be identified later at school.

Older children can collect leaves and see what effect dirt has had on them. If the leaves are wiped with damp towels the amount of dirt can be seen, and children can discuss how this might affect the growth of the tree.

Looking at street trees the children can see how well they are cared for. Have notices been nailed onto the trunk? Have they been badly trimmed? Are the paving stones too close (has the tree room for growth)? Are the trees in such a position that the trunks are scarred by passing traffic? Have vandals damaged the trees in any way? Are the trees suitable for town growth?

Children are used to seeing cats and dogs and they could make a count of these. This could include some work on the care of cats and dogs, and a discussion as to the reasons why dogs should not be allowed to run loose in streets. The R.S.P.C.A. have leaflets and films on the care of cats and dogs and some of these are suitable for very young children. If asked, parents would probably be willing to bring a cat or dog to school so that the children could look at it carefully and talk about the care of the animal.

The oldest infants could make a reasonable survey of the whole area around the school. This could include counting plants and animals, grouping these according to where found, making plans to show positions of trees and noting any interesting finds. Photographs would be useful here and could show such things as plants growing on walls, tree damage in streets, the layout of parks, street trees, birds feeding etc. This cannot be as accurate as such a study would be with older children but it can make infants aware of their surroundings, and they could show their findings to other children, parents and local people.

Specific studies could be undertaken by groups of children, e.g.

trees in the roads near school
plants found in the school grounds
rubbish, and what it does to the surroundings
making a bird table
a survey of Rosebay Willow Herb
looking at the park
plants and railway bridges
the effect of dirt on the trees in the town
looking at town weeds
plants on walls and buildings
a survey of the street (this could include history, environmental studies and local biology)
street names that tell us about the past.

SUPPORT MATERIAL

Books for the children

In the Park H. Wigley (Ginn)
Autumn Trees Irene Finch (Longmans)
What You Can Find in a Park Clare Williams (A. and C. Black)
Conservation James Whinray (A. and C. Black)
Wild Flowers of Verges and Waste Land Jean Imrie (A. and C. Black)
Exploring the Park Leslie Jackman (Evans)
Exploring the Garden Leslie Jackman (Evans)

Books for teacher reference

The Ecology of Towns Alfred Leutscher (Franklin Watts)
Street Flowers Richard Mabey (Kestrel Books)
Looking Around in Town and Country Philip Sauvain (Franklin Watts)
Early Explorations Science 5/13 (Macdonald Educational)
An *A to Z* or street guide of the local area.

Useful apparatus

Camera; tape measure; trundle wheel; hand-lens; plastic boxes and bags; trowel; pooter* for collecting small animals; large sheets of squared paper, slides showing animals likely to be seen in towns; wood for a simple bird table; strings of peanuts; wax crayons; local maps (for teacher reference).

*(See diagram page 118.)

A pooter

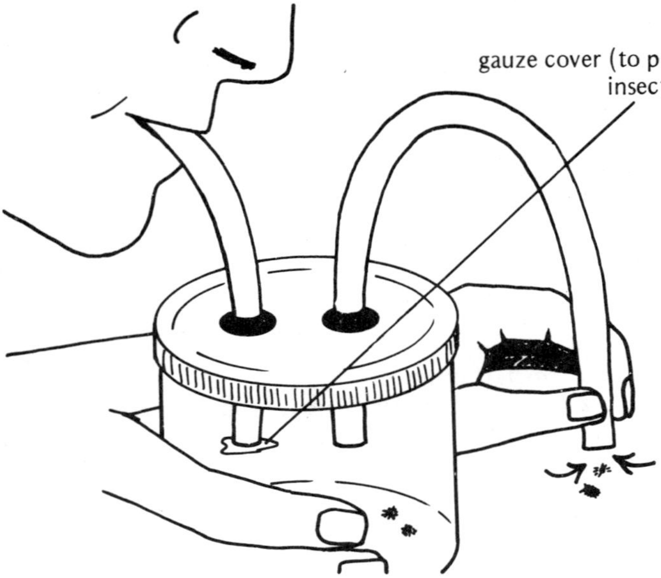

20 WET WEATHER

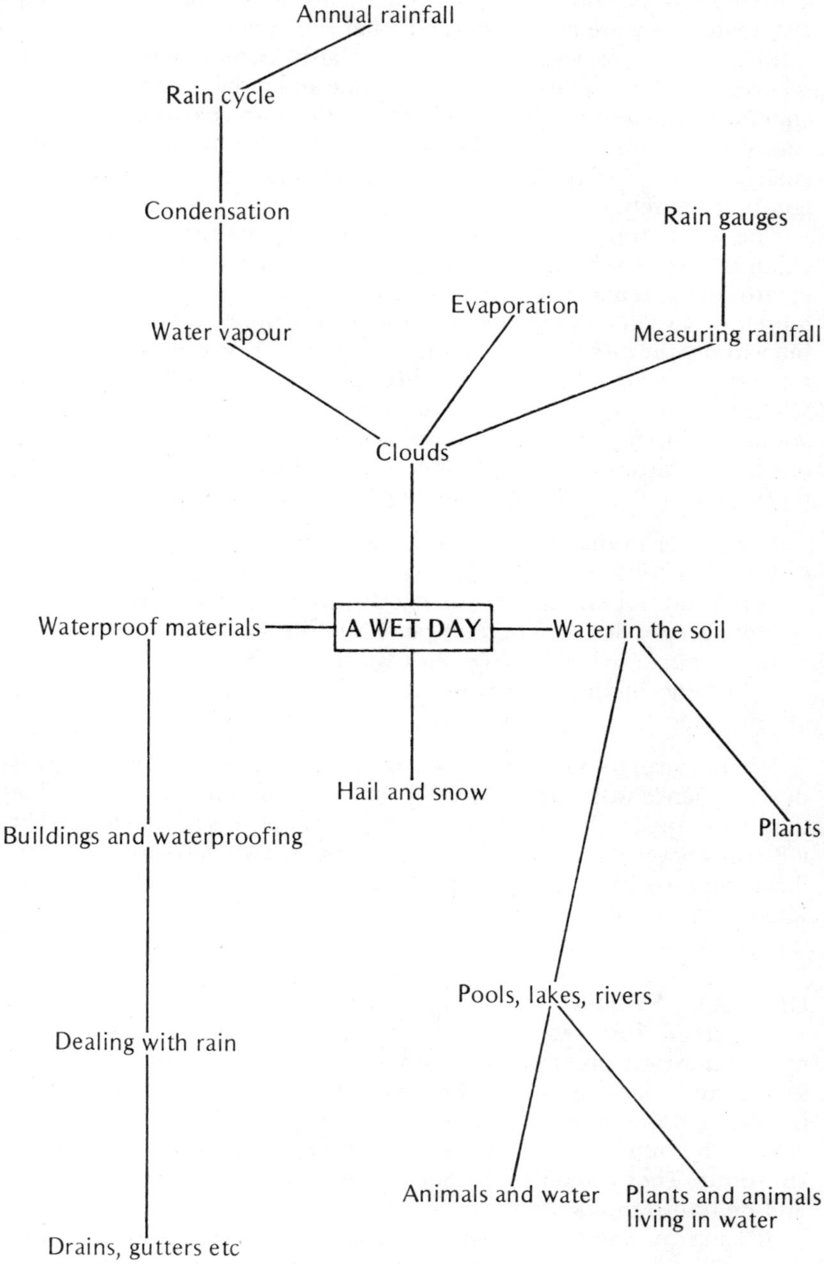

Weather is a topic familiar to all of us, and even the youngest children make observations about it. They know that warm and cold days, rainy and sunny days, snowy and windy days are important because they affect what they are able to do and what they wear.

Keeping simple weather records is fairly common in all infant schools, but this can develop into a routine and rather boring job. One child, each day, is usually deputed to put the correct symbol — rainy, sunny etc — onto the weather chart or board (though it is rarely changed if conditions alter during the day!) and most of the others ignore it entirely.

The whole topic can become much more interesting and alive if children can be shown how much weather affects them and their environment. It may be a nuisance that it is raining at playtime and they therefore have to stay indoors when they would much rather be outside, but without the rain the plants would not grow! They can do some basic weather recording but even at this early stage it should be more scientific than a mere observation of apparent conditions. Even very young children can use a simple wind indicator, a rain gauge (measuring arbitrarily — calibrated gauges can come later) and a thermometer. They can also investigate various problems:

Is it cooler in the shade or in the sun?
What happens on a windy day? What sort of things get blown about?
Is the sun hot enough to warm a dish of water put outside?
How deeply does falling rain penetrate the soil?
If you put snow in a refrigerator will it turn into ice?
How long will the sun stay out (within a given time, say, during the morning)?

Wet days can be a source of ideas on which children can base a great deal of science work, and this will prove to be much more acceptable than a topic just called 'Water'. The study of water, as such, is so vast that it is really beyond the capabilities of infants, and will have to be broken down into workable topics, e.g. 'Water in the home', 'How we use water', 'Water and growing plants', 'Animals living in water' or 'Wet day things'.

GENERAL NOTES

1 Weather involves cloud, rainfall and humidity; sun and temperature; air pressure and winds. Conditions vary from season to season and place to place. The water cycle is a continuous process involving evaporation and condensation — both difficult concepts for young children and the words themselves have no really adequate substitute. They can only be made to understand the meanings by use and demonstration.

A saucer of water will 'disappear' gradually (more quickly in warm, dry weather) because it has evaporated. It has become water vapour in the air. A 'mist' of tiny droplets forms on a glass of very cold water if we breathe on it, or leave it outside for a while. The water vapour in the air has condensed, and changed back into droplets.

2 Rain water comes indirectly from the sea (since this occupies such a large area of the earth's surface it is, therefore, the source of most water evaporation). The water evaporates, forming vapour in the atmosphere. As this rises and cools it condenses into droplets which form clouds; moving air carries these clouds overland where further cooling results in the formation of larger drops. These fall to the earth as rain. Rain flows through the ground, gradually forming springs as it meets the impervious layers of rock, and these feed the the streams and rivers which ultimately flow into the sea

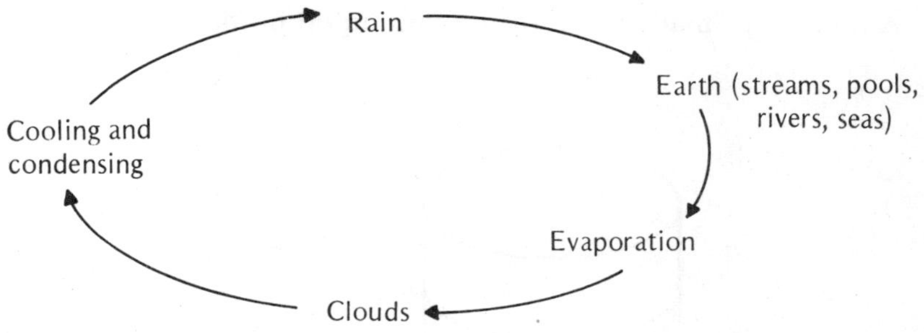

3 The water content of the soil varies according to the composition of the soil, and the amount and depth of rock layers. Clay soils, composed of tiny particles, become waterlogged as the particles cling together. Soils containing humus absorb and retain water, but they also have plenty of air spaces. Water finds its own level with its surface forming a horizontal line. This happens in soil, the level being known as the 'water table'. Where a lake or pool is formed the water table is above ground (the surface level of the pool). Marshes show that the water table is at ground level.

4 All plants and animals are dependent on rainfall, and without water all living organisms would die. Germination and growth of seeds depend on the availability of water; small plants get their water from the top soil, and large plants, such as trees, reach down to the water trapped deep below the surface. Some plants and animals live entirely in water, and most obtain their oxygen from this water. The fresh water organisms depend on rainfall to keep sufficient water in pools, lakes, ponds, rivers and streams. The sea is constantly fed by the water from the rivers flowing into it.

5 Waterproofing is important if plants and animals — including humans — are to withstand rain. Feathers are waterproof (watch a Duck diving for food). Leaves and bark absorb little water, and shiny leaves, such as Holly, are completely impervious.

Man needs to waterproof his home, wear waterproof materials, protect wood and metal from wet, produce road surfaces that can withstand rain and which do not disintegrate in water.

PLANNING AND PREPARATION

1 Make simple rain gauges with washing-up bottles. Pull off the loose nozzle and cut the top off the bottle about one third of the way down. Invert this top part into the bottom part. The children can tip the rain water this 'gauge' catches into a straight jar (such as an Alka-seltzer bottle) and can mark the level of water on a strip of paper stuck down the side. Obviously this will not give an accurate measure of rainfall, but it can be used for comparison.

A rain gauge made from washing-up liquid bottles

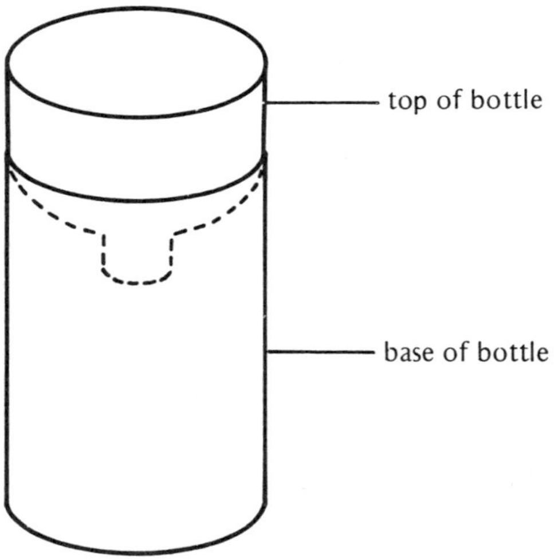

2 Wind indicators can be made by using strips (22 cm x 4 cm) of various materials and suspending these loosely from a taut length of string or wire, by thread loops through holes bored at one end of each strip. If the strips are made of paper, thin card, polystyrene tile, thick card, plywood, thicker wood etc, it can be noted which strips move. The lighter materials will move easily in a light breeze and so on. Children can devise their own experiments with this simple apparatus.

A wind gauge

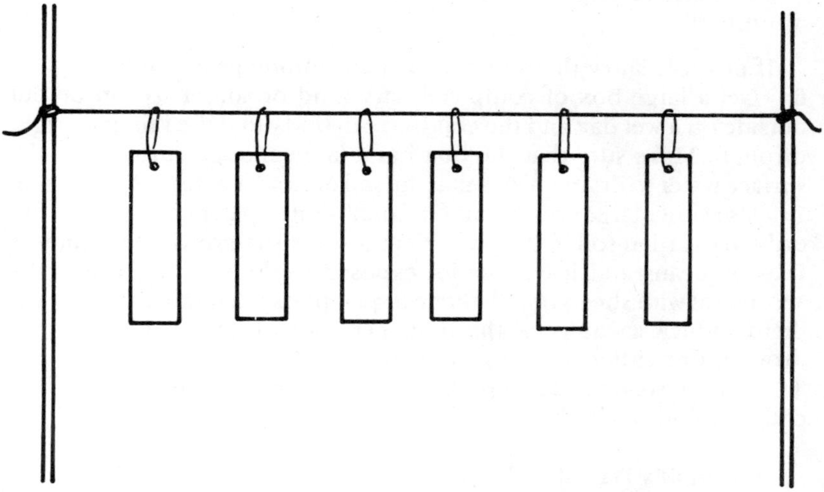

3 Various materials can be collected to test if they are waterproof. These can be cut so that they will go over the top of, say, an empty bean tin (with the top removed with a rotary cutter) and fixed with a rubber band. All the tins and their materials can then be watered with a watering can with a rose. The children can then see which materials have let the water through. Test polythene, rubber sheeting, metal foil, loosely woven cotton material, firmly woven cotton, nylon, denim, gaberdine, knitted wool, paper etc. Experiment to see if material that is stretched tightly is more waterproof than material left loose (show the children an umbrella).

4 Collect together building materials such as bricks, tiles and slates. If a brick is placed in a bowl of water it will absorb a great deal of the water, and children can see this. They can be shown the damp course of the school building or a house, and can try to see how water is prevented from rising up a house wall. If one brick is half immersed in water and another is put on top the water will eventually rise through both of them. If the same experiment is repeated, but a sheet of roof-felt or polythene is put inbetween, the top brick stays dry. Roofing materials can be looked at and discussed – tiles, slates, tarred felt, corrugated iron, plastic and thatch. Ways of treating wood so that it will not rot can be looked at and children can experiment with oil, paint and creosote to see if they will waterproof wood.

5 Get a complete set of waterproof clothes so that children can see the advantages of wearing all or some of these:

wellingtons
macintosh or cycle cape
anorak

waterproof trousers
souwester or other waterproof hat
umbrella.

If possible show them underwater swimming gear (a wet suit).

6 Get a large box of completely dry sand or soil. This can be put outside on a wet day and the children can find out if the rain goes right through. Make sure that the box has a large enough surface for the surface water to drain off and that the soil or sand is at least 20 cm deep.

7 Use either large flower pots (12" or 30 cm) or patches of garden. Put ordinary garden soil in the pots. Plant some easily-grown seeds such as Peas or Beans and leave one lot exposed to the weather. Cover the second lot with sheets of polythene or perspex so that rain cannot get at them. Which seeds grow the best? (Try not to do this in a time of drought or neither set will germinate!)

8 Collect weather sayings. Use these for discussion, and let the children find out if they are true, e.g.

St Swithin's Day, if it should rain,
For forty days it will remain.

Red sky at night; a shepherd's delight,
Red sky in the morning; a shepherd's warning.

(Is this a warning of rain to come?)

They can try and find out other weather sayings for themselves.

WORKING AND RECORDING

The youngest children can look at the effects of rain on themselves, on the buildings and on the things around them. Dress one child in wet weather clothes and ask why he wears special things when it is raining; stand wellingtons in a bowl of water and show that the insides keep dry; using a watering can with a rose, sprinkle an umbrella and a waterproof coat, and then try the same thing on, say, a cotton dress. Which lets the water go through? Which would it be best to wear on a rainy day? Make a composite picture of 'A Wet Day'. Show umbrellas, boots, macs etc.

After a rain storm look at puddles. What happens to them after the rain has stopped? Where does the water go? Some will evaporate, and some will soak into the ground. Let the children set up some simple experiments to show that rain will sink into soil and turf better than into stone, concrete and tarmac.

Some of the children can test to see which materials are waterproof. Examples of the materials can be stuck on a chart after being sorted into sets of waterproof materials, materials that let water through and materials which only let a little water through. This can be followed by a look at the waterproofing necessary for a building. Children can see why a roof should prevent rain from seeping through and could try various different things to see if they would be suitable for roofing. They can see how tiles are laid, and could find out, using a few tiles, what would happen if they were placed so that water could get between them. Other things they could look at on a building are guttering, drains and paintwork. A model house could be made showing:

a sloping roof — the rain will run off it
guttering (cardboard tubes cut in half) — to stop water running down the walls
drainpipes — to carry water from the gutters to the drains
paintwork — to seal wood and stop it absorbing water
windows made of glass — to let light through, and to keep out water and draught.

Weather recording can include some information on rainfall. Using simple rain gauges rain water can be collected. This can either be put into test tubes or jars (corked) each day and labelled with the date so that the amount of water can be compared, or it can be measured by pouring it into an Alka-seltzer bottle and marking, on a piece of paper stuck on the side, where it comes to each day. This will not give an accurate measurement of rainfall, but will give an indication of 'the wettest day', 'the day with least rain' etc.

Older children can try experiments to see what will happen to plants if they cannot get sufficient water. Pea seeds can be planted in pots and some can be watered (artificial rain) and others left unwatered. The children can record their findings and decide which conditions suit seeds best. If patches of garden are available similar experiments can be tried. Seeds such as Radishes can be planted. Plot A can be in the open, where it will be rained on, and Plot B can be covered in some way so that no rain reaches it.

Water can be put into various containers and left. Which evaporates first? If the same amount of water is put in each container will the water in a flat open dish evaporate before the water in a tall narrow container? It is not easy for young children to appreciate that the water does not vanish entirely but becomes part of the atmosphere, but they can see that it disappears from the container.

Once the children have realized that rain is essential for growing plants they can find out something about soil water. Ask them if they can think of ways of finding out how far rain will sink into the ground, and how quickly soil dries out. If they dig in soil after a period of drought they can see how dry it is. How far down is it dry? Where do the growing plants get their water in these conditions? Where do trees get water?

A class could put on a 'Wet Weather' exhibition. This could include the results of their experiments, weather records, samples of wet weather clothing, pictures of houses showing where they are waterproofed, creative writing about rain, poems, pictures and songs (the latter on tape so that they can be played back).

SUPPORT MATERIAL

Books for the children:

Weather Starters Series (Macdonald Educational)
The Weather (6 small books) Jean Wilson (Chambers)
Weather First Library Series (Macdonald Educational)
Water First Library Series (Macdonald Educational)

Books for teacher reference

Early Experiences Science 5/13 (Macdonald Educational)
General Science Book 3 Charles Windridge (Schofield & Sims)
Tackling Problems Part 2 Science 5/13 (Macdonald Educational)

Useful apparatus

Washing-up liquid bottles; containers of different shapes and sizes; pieces of material; slates; tiles; bricks; polythene sheeting; rubber sheeting; Alka-seltzer bottles; test tubes; watering can (with rose); dry sand or soil; Pea seeds; flower pots.

21 SUMMER DAYS

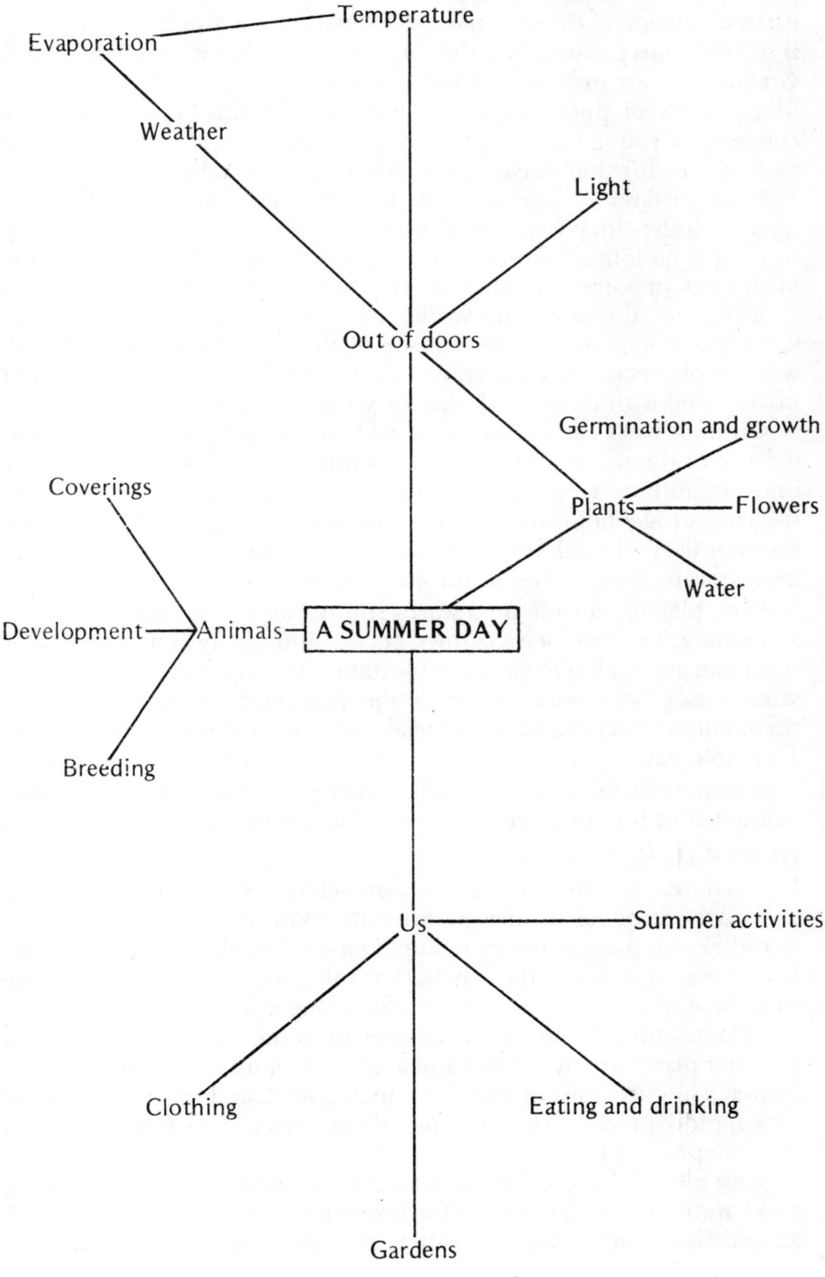

If children look at the sun they will see that it is in different positions at different times of the day. They will also know that it does not shine when there is a great deal of cloud about or at night, but they will probably not realize that night and day depend on the position of the earth in relation to the sun, and that even when the sun is not obvious it is still the source of light. On the sun, too, depends the growth of plants. Green plants are only able to manufacture food in the presence of light (the process of photosynthesis) and although this is too difficult a concept for young children, they can experiment with growing plants and can see for themselves the effects of lack of light.

Summer days are also warmer. The children can tell this from the type of clothes they wear, the flowers in the gardens and the fact that heating is no longer necessary at home and at school. Because of the likelihood of better weather there are far more opportunities for children to do outdoor work, and they can develop simple investigations for themselves. Some of these can be concerned with weather observations, temperature and plant growth, and will often fit in very well with other work that they may be doing.

Outdoor work can usefully be used to introduce the older infants to the use of the thermometer, and it is not necessary for them to fully understand how a thermometer works to appreciate that a rise in the mercury or alcohol level indicates that it is warmer. A clear, outdoor thermometer should be used and the children should learn that temperature is measured in units called degrees.

Even playing outside on a warm sunny day will teach the children something. They will see shadows, get hot and thirsty and find out that stone can get too hot to sit on comfortably. This is another topic where science can be carried out with the minimum of apparatus, and preparations can be made well ahead so that work can be carried out on a suitable day.

'Summer Days' as a topic offers scope for not only science and mathematics but art work, creative writing, poetry etc.

GENERAL NOTES

1 As the earth travels around the sun each year it spins on its own axis, and it is the tilt of this axis that governs our seasons. At different times of the year different parts of the earth are tilted towards the sun, and in June Britain is at its closest to the sun. In December it is at its furthest from the sun; the days are shorter and the nights longer, any sunshine is weak.

2 Plants and animals adapt themselves to the changing seasons. In summer plants are in full leaf and are building up reserves of food for winter. They are flowering and producing seed, and those which grow very rapidly produce several generations during the summer months (e.g. Shepherd's Purse).

With plentiful vegetation animals can feed well during the summer, and conditions are favourable for breeding. The hair and fur of most animals is less thick than in winter, and there may be other obvious changes, e.g. colourful plumage of some male birds, colour changes in Newts etc.

The life cycles of many insects are fairly short in warm weather when food is easy to obtain, e.g. Houseflies, many Butterflies, Ladybirds. Bees etc are active and are storing honey for winter feeding.

3 Children can be shown that the position of the sun in the sky varies during the day. (N.B. Children should be told never to look directly at the sun. If they want to do so they should be given *very* dark glasses).* Shadows give an indication of the position of the sun in the sky. When the sun is low, as in the evening, the shadows will be long, and when it is overhead, at midday, they will be short and clearly outlined.

4 When the weather is warm and the air is not humid washing will dry in a very short time because the water in it evaporates quickly. Water will also evaporate from ponds and pools, and water left in flat dishes soon disappears. In time of prolonged drought there is considerable danger to wild life in ponds and streams, and plants with short roots penetrating only the surface layers will die unless they are watered.

5 Plants rely on sunlight to manufacture their food. Using light energy the water (taken in by the roots) and the carbon dioxide (taken in by the leaves) are built up into complex substances. Without light plants will die. Children do not need to understand photosynthesis but they can see that all life on earth depends on plants either directly or indirectly. Plant-eating animals feed on vegetation (on land or in water). Other animals feed on the plant eaters. Some of the simpler food chains can be discussed and it can be shown that all living organisms rely on plants, e.g.

Green leaves→Caterpillars→Birds
Grass→Cows→Producing milk→Us
Grass→Rabbits→Foxes

6 Although young children like instant results photographs can be used to show seasonal changes. If there is a tree, a park or some woodland nearby (where the children can see it easily) photographs can be taken in the winter, spring, summer and autumn so that these can be compared. If each photograph is taken from exactly the same place the children will be able to recognize the seasonal changes and understand that each time of the year affects plants differently.

WORKING AND RECORDING

1 On a sunny day children can investigate shadows. The youngest children can look at these; they can try to run away from their own shadow and can see if their shadow always copies them exactly. They can play a game chasing shadows and try to 'capture' someone else's shadow by standing on it. Ask them questions such as:

What is the longest shadow you can make?

*For example, several layers of dark film.

What is the smallest shadow?
Can you run away from your shadow?
Can you go to a place where your shadow cannot be seen?
Can you touch your own shadow?
Can you stand on your friend's shadow?
Can you stand with your shadow in front of you?

Gradually they should realize that they will only have a shadow when there is sunshine. Once they get into the shade it disappears, and so shadows depend on light.

Older children can draw round shadows — either on the playground or on a large piece of paper. If they draw round the shadow of one of the children they can then stand him in exactly the same place some hours later. Is the shadow still the same size? Can they explain why the length of the shadow has altered?

Are shadows always the same shape as the object they are shadowing? Children can try making shadows with a variety of objects to find this out.

A simple shadow clock can be made using a jumping stand or a garden cane held upright in a flower pot of stones. if this is placed in the playground, chalk lines can mark the positions of the shadows during the day. Is the shadow line in the same place at playtime (say, 10.45) every day?

A simple shadow clock

If possible show the children a sundial, and discuss how it could be used to tell the time. See if they realize why it would be useless at night, on sunless days and during most of the winter. This could lead to further work on time, and different instruments used to indicate the time of day:

shadow clocks
water and sand clocks
candle clocks
mechanical clocks.

Time is not an easy concept for young children but they can be introduced, gradually, to divisions of the day, the idea of 'yesterday' and 'tomorrow', weeks, months and years.

2 If they are doing weather studies they will have already been introduced to recording such things as sunny and wet days. Older children can make some recordings of temperature and these can be compared over, say, one week, e.g.

outdoor temperature at playtime each morning
temperature at dinner-time in the playground, both in the sun and in the shade.

They can be asked if they can think of other ways of showing that the weather is warmer. (Water in a dish gets warm; the ground feels warm; clothes are thinner and lighter.)

3 Using a mail order catalogue children can cut out and collect summer clothes, and can be asked why they have chosen those particular clothes. A large card outline of a child can be 'dressed' in clothes drawn, coloured, and cut out by the children showing suitable clothing for warmer weather. This can be altered according to the weather outside, e.g. a raincoat can be put on on a wet day. If each cut-out paper garment has hooks made from paper clips the clothes can be changed easily.

4 Summer is an ideal time for children to grow plants. Seeds that germinate quickly (see Section 3) are always best for young children and they can experiment by growing them in different conditions. For example, using small flower pots with soil or seed compost, plant seeds such as Radishes. Treat the pots in various ways, e.g.

having planted them do not water them again
put one pot in the sunniest part of the playground and put another in a place that is always shady
put one in a refrigerator (if possible).

5 As plants need light some simple experiments can be done to show this.

a Plant Mustard seeds in two pots. Keep both watered but put one in a cupboard in the dark and put the other in a light place. The children can see what happens to the plants as they grow. Those in the dark will grow long and spindly, with yellow leaves (etiolation) and those in the light will be green and healthy.

b Well-established plants can be placed on a window sill and not turned round. All the leaves will grow towards the light. If a plant such as a Geranium is used it can be seen that the leaves will position themselves so that they get the maximum light. When doing this with children it is best to mark the pots in some way (a dab of paint to show the side of the pot away from the light) as they are sure to move them to look at them.

6 People wear sunglasses in the summer. Children can wear sunglasses to see if things look different with tinted glass. They can look at bright things — a white wall, shiny metal — in sunlight and see if it is easier to look at them wearing the glasses. (Again, stress the importance of not looking directly at the sun.) The power of the sun's rays can be demonstrated using a magnifying glass to focus the rays onto a piece of paper. The children will see the paper burn. Although this not an experiment young children should be encouraged to try, it can be used to show one of the dangers of leaving bottles about. The curved surface of the bottle acts in the same way as the magnifying glass, and heath and hedgerow fires can be started very easily if bottles or broken glass are left about.

WORKING AND RECORDING

The youngest children can talk about shadows. They can tell you what happened when they went outside in the sun, and the results of the various games they tried out. This could be taped so that there is a permanent record of the work done. It is also interesting to ask young children to draw themselves and their shadows. Very few will draw the shadow touching the picture of themselves, and even if asked to look again will be unable to grasp this aspect.

The outline shadow pictures (if done on paper) can be cut out and made into a large wall picture showing the size at different times of the day, and children can try making shadow pictures with their hands.

Any plant experiments can be labelled and short explanations added either in writing or on tape. These can be included with a general survey of plants in summer — leaves on trees, flowers, insects visiting flowers, need for water in very dry weather, speed of growth etc.

A general topic on 'Summer' can be shown in various ways, e.g.:

a summer clothes model
a frieze of summer activities — sports, bathing, paddling, sunbathing, caravanning, sailing, cutting wheat etc
a weather chart showing fine days and sunny days
a temperature chart
sundials and shadow clocks
animals in summer — thinner coats on Dogs and Cats, brighter

feathers on birds, more insects about, larvae of insects to be found, Squirrels to be seen, more farm animals in the fields etc
pictures, done by children, to show their own ideas of summer
poems and songs about summer days
a collection of 'sun' words, with pictures — sun, sunrise, sunset, sunshine, sunbathing, sunflower, sunburn, sunglasses, sun-hat, sunshade etc.

Older children can make temperature charts showing the temperature each day over some weeks, and can find out if it is cooler in the shade than it is in the sunshine. They can devise ways of judging this without using a thermometer, and can try and find out what is the hottest part of the day. If tiles or slates are wetted and put in different places they can see how quickly they dry, and which dries first. With this they can do some work on evaporation. If the dolls' clothes are washed they can try to decide where they will dry best, and which sort of day is best for washing clothes.

For those who are reading, simple work cards posing particular problems can be made:

> Measure your friend's shadow on a sunny day.
> Measure from his feet to the head of the shadow.
>
> At 10 o'clock it was . . . cm long.
>
> At 11 o'clock it was . . . cm long.
>
> At 12 o'clock it was . . . cm long.
>
> At 1 o'clock it was . . . cm long.
>
> At 2 o'clock it was . . . cm long.
>
> The shadow was longest at . . . o'clock.
>
> The shadow was shortest at . . . o'clock.

> Go outside.
>
> Write down all the things you see that show you that it is summer.
>
> These will help you to begin:
>
> The windows are all open.
>
> The sun is out.
>
> - - - - - - - - - - - - -
>
> - - - - - - - - - - - - -
>
> - - - - - - - - - - - - -
>
> - - - - - - - - - - - - -
>
> - - - - - - - - - - - - -

SUPPORT MATERIAL

Books for the children
Animals in the Summer Vera Croxford (Transworld Publishers)
What to Look for in Summer E. L. Grant-Watson (Ladybird Books)

Books for teacher reference
Early Experiences Science 5/13 (Macdonald Educational)
Science from the Beginning Book 1 B. L. Hampson and K. C. Evans (Oliver and Boyd)
Early Explorations Science 5/13 (Macdonald Educational)
The Puffin Book of Gardening Mary Kelly (Puffin Books)

Useful apparatus
Flower pots; sunglasses; tinted glass; seeds; plants (growing in pots); camera; garden canes; chalk; large sheets of paper; outdoor thermometers; magnifying glass; old mail order catalogues.

22 COLLECTING THINGS: WHAT TO COLLECT

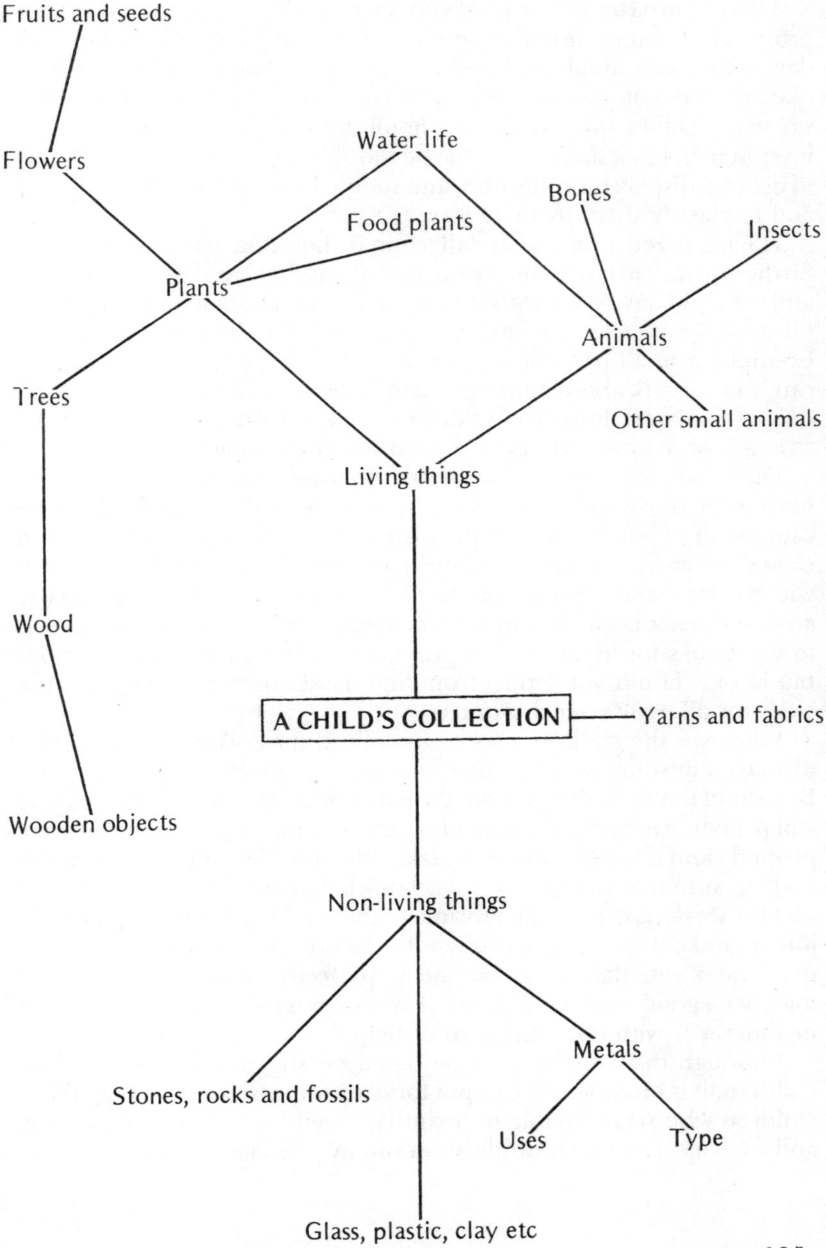

Children like collecting things; with very little encouragement they will pick up stones, shells, grasses, boxes, labels and so on. Any offers of cards or plastic toys given away with sweets or breakfast cereal will ensure a steady sale while the offer lasts!

This enthusiasm can be used very successfully for the start of science projects but unless the collections have a definite purpose they will soon degenerate into unlabelled and unidentified groups of objects which may, or may not, have something in common. This does not mean to say that a child's own collection should be so structured that he loses interest in it, but it does mean that he should be given every opportunity to use and display his collection, and should be helped to identify things and to classify them in some way.

Having made a particular collection it should be used as a basis for further work. This may simply mean that it is displayed well, is labelled and the child has a chance to tell his class mates about it; or it may spark off a whole trail of new and exciting work for the whole class. For example, a small collection of shells, probably picked up at random, can lead to work about animals which have shells, a study of snails or a deeper study of shore life. Older children may use them to test the strength of natural objects or to find out something about spirals.

Obviously reference books should be used, and many of these will have to be those with a far higher reading level than the children are capable of coping with, but providing the pictures are accurate and clear this hardly matters. It will mean that the children need more help with the texts and explanations but it is an opportunity for them to use good reference books and to learn to handle these sensibly. Teach them to use books for identification purposes and for further information; but books should not detract from first-hand observation which is the basis for all early science work.

Whatever the children choose to collect, the collections should be displayed in some way, together with any work stemming from them. Be careful not to underestimate the enthusiasm that will be shown; you will probably need a great deal of room to display a good piece of work properly and if the children have taken the trouble to do this it is worth making sure that they get some acknowledgment.

This work has, also, the advantage that children of all abilities can join in and compete successfully with the others. The non-reader may need help with labelling, but he is perfectly capable of gathering together a good collection of, say, leaves or grasses and mounting them in some way with the minimum of help.

Although this work should be based on suggestions made by the children, it is often sensible to put forward some 'starters' to help those children who seem unable to formulate their own ideas at this stage, and to avoid too much duplication in any one classroom.

GENERAL NOTES

It is impossible to make a comprehensive list of all the suitable collections for young children. Every teacher will have different ideas according to locality, opportunity and the ability and age of the children concerned, but the following should give some idea of the very wide variety of topics, and these can be adapted to suit individual needs. Children should also be taught something about conservation (see 'Rules for collectors' on page 139).

1 Collections of flowers:

a general collection of wild flowers either identified, labelled and kept alive in water for a short time, or pressed and mounted
b specialized collections of flowers, e.g. flowers from waste land, roadside verges, coastland or the edge of the school field
c flowers of the month – a collection of wild flowers seen during one particular month
d garden weeds.

2 Leaves can be collected as live specimens, pressed, used for leaf rubbings or cast with plaster of paris.

3 Bark rubbings.

4 Specialized tree collection: Use any one tree and make a collection of all the things concerned with it, e.g. leaf and bark rubbings, twig casts in plaster of paris, example of the fruit, drawings of any insects found on the leaves or bark (caterpillars can be kept in suitable containers), drawings of any birds or animals visiting the tree, sample of the same type of wood, examples of things made from this wood (see Section 7).

5 Fruits and seeds: This could include a collection of seed packets if children want to start this in the spring.

6 Grasses: These are not easy to identify but as many different species as possible can be collected and displayed to show the number to be found in a relatively small area.

7 Food plants: Examples of root vegetables, cereals and some fruits can be kept for a reasonable length of time, but many food plants are not suitable for long-term display. After children have seen examples they will either have to make drawings or collect pictures, but they should be given the opportunity to see as many as possible. We sometimes forget that some children have never seen food plants growing in their natural state and this work should give them the chance to see, at least, a few of these.

8 Caterpillars (see Section 8) and other small animals (see Section 9).

9 Water life: This is a collection that will have to be kept in a suitable tank of some sort but preparing this can be the most interesting part of the work for many children.

10 Shore life: Sea-water aquaria are not easy to maintain and should only be attempted if you are confident that water is easily available and you have some knowledge of their upkeep. Children can collect shells,

stones, seaweeds, sea shore plants and any of the interesting things found on the shore. A collection of things brought back from holidays by town children will often provide the material for a display.

11 Bones can be collected from fields, heaths, seashores etc or can be the remains of Sunday's dinner (i.e. poultry bones). They are not always easy to identify but children like collecting bones and will often provide the most unlikely specimens if asked to look out for them during a school holiday.

12 Animals in the garden (or school grounds). Although such small animals as spiders and ladybirds can be kept for a short time most of this collection will have to be in the form of drawings and pictures, but it has the advantage that it can be added to as new specimens are found. This collection, in a suburban school, included Sparrows, Starlings, Wagtails, Blue Tits, a Seagull, Wood Pigeons, three types of Spider, Wasps, Honey Bees, Bumble Bees, Ladybirds, Violet Ground Beetles, Earthworms, Small Tortoiseshell caterpillars, Earwigs, Woodlice, Houseflies, several other (un-named) flies, domestic Cat, Small White Butterfly and Ants.

13 Rocks, stones and fossils: Young children will not be able to identify different rocks but they like collecting stones. These can be grouped according to colour, shape or where found but they will introduce children to the idea that all rock is not the same.

14 Yarns and fabrics

A zig-zag book used for displaying a collection

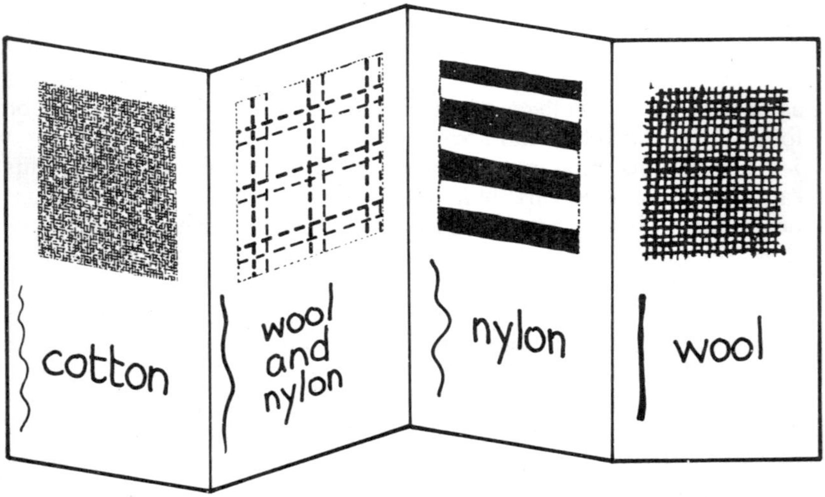

15 Tools: This can either be a specialized collection, e.g. tools connected with carpentry, cooking, gardening etc, or can be a general collection to show that a tool is something for making a particular task

easier. Once this has been discussed the children can make this collection themselves from things found at home and at school. After the more ordinary things (scissors, needle, pencil, knife, spoon, hammer, pliers, spade etc) have been seen it should be possible to put together a collection of old or unusual tools.

16 Woods and wooden objects

17 Metal things

18 Building materials: Wood, bricks, tiles, slates, cement, concrete, nails, glass etc.

19 Paper: Examples of different types of paper.

20 Packaging: Boxes, jars, bottles, plastic tubs, paper and foil wrappings, plastic bags etc.

21 Postage stamps: Thematic collections of stamps showing plants or animals on them.

22 Unusual or interesting things, i.e. things that are interesting and unusual to the children. One class of seven year olds included in their collection of 'Interesting Things' an oak apple, a very large nail, a stone with a hole in it, a painted flower pot, a wire puzzle, a crab shell, a bird's skull and a broken clock, but each child had a reason for including his particular contribution.

23 Collections based on particular themes of colour or shape, e.g. symmetrical things, spherical things, triangular things, blue things, spirals.

PLANNING AND PREPARATION

1 Before children start collecting — particularly living material — they should be taught some 'Rules for collectors':

a Never damage trees in any way.

b Never pull plants out of the ground.

c If flowers are being collected the children should be told to collect one only — and any rare plants should be looked at and then left alone.

d If stones, logs etc are moved see that they are put back in exactly the same place. Every stone may conceal a mini-environment, and careless collecting may destroy it.

e Conservation is very important. If, for example, frog spawn is being collected it is quite unnecessary to remove the whole clump. Take about twenty eggs; this will be sufficient for classroom study. When the tadpoles have begun to change into frogs return them to the pond again.

f Never disturb nesting birds and never take eggs from nests. In many cases the birds are protected, and it is illegal to take eggs.

g Insects etc are far better studied alive. There is no need to kill them. Caterpillars and other small animals can be kept quite easily if they are housed and fed properly.

2 If children are going out to collect things they will need suitable containers to put specimens in, e.g.

plastic bags, large and small
margarine pots with lids (perforated if they are likely to collect small animals)
a basket or trug for grasses and flowers — these soon wilt if they are held in hot hands
a small trowel and a suitable box if small seedlings (Sycamore, Oak etc) are to be dug up for planting later
black, wax crayons and strong, thin paper for bark and leaf rubbings
a strong bag for stones and rocks
a fishing net and watertight plastic pots for pond and stream dipping
plastic boxes for delicate specimens — bones, crab shells, fungi.

(N.B. Children should not collect fungi without asking you first. If you are not sure which are poisonous leave well alone.) Older children will need pencils and small note books to write down where each specimen was found.

3 Preserving collections:

a Leaves and flowers can be pressed between sheets of blotting paper and several thicknesses of newspaper. These need to be placed under a heavy weight for some weeks. Alternatively a press can be made with two thick pieces of plywood and two heavy G-clamps. The pressed specimens can be mounted with tiny strips of Sellotape, or can be placed on card and covered with adhesive laminating sheeting.

b Stones and shells will show up their colours better if they are painted with clear varnish.

c Many fruits, grasses, seeds and twigs can be mounted or put in boxes straightaway.

d If bones are not already clean and dry they should be boiled with a little detergent until all the fat has been removed, and then dried in the oven or a warm place.

4 For many collections the cooperation of parents will be useful and if they are asked to produce things it is sensible to ask them to see the final collection, and the work derived from it.

WORKING AND RECORDING

See Section 23 *Working with Collections.*

SUPPORT MATERIAL

Books for the children

Collecting Things Romola Showell (Ward Lock Educational)

Collecting Things Starters Series (Macdonald Educational)
Weeds Mollie Clarke (Hart-Davis)
Caterpillars Mollie Clarke (Hart-Davis)
Trees Mollie Clarke (Hart-Davis)
Butterflies, Moths and Other Insects S. A. Manning (Ladybird Books)
Exploring the Garden Leslie Jackman (Evans)
The Seashore and Seashore Life Nancy Scott (Ladybird Books)

Books for teacher reference
Any good book of wild flowers.
The Observer's Book of Pond Life John Clegg (Warne)
Wild Flowers of Verges and Waste Land Jean Imrie (A. and C. Black)
Early Explorations Science 5/13 (Macdonald Educational)
Rocks and Minerals H. S. Zimm and P. R. Shaffer (Paul Hamlyn)
The Oxford Book of Invertebrates David Nichols and John Cooke (OUP)

Useful apparatus
Pots; boxes and bags for collecting; hand-lenses; camera; trowel.

23 COLLECTING THINGS: WORKING WITH COLLECTIONS

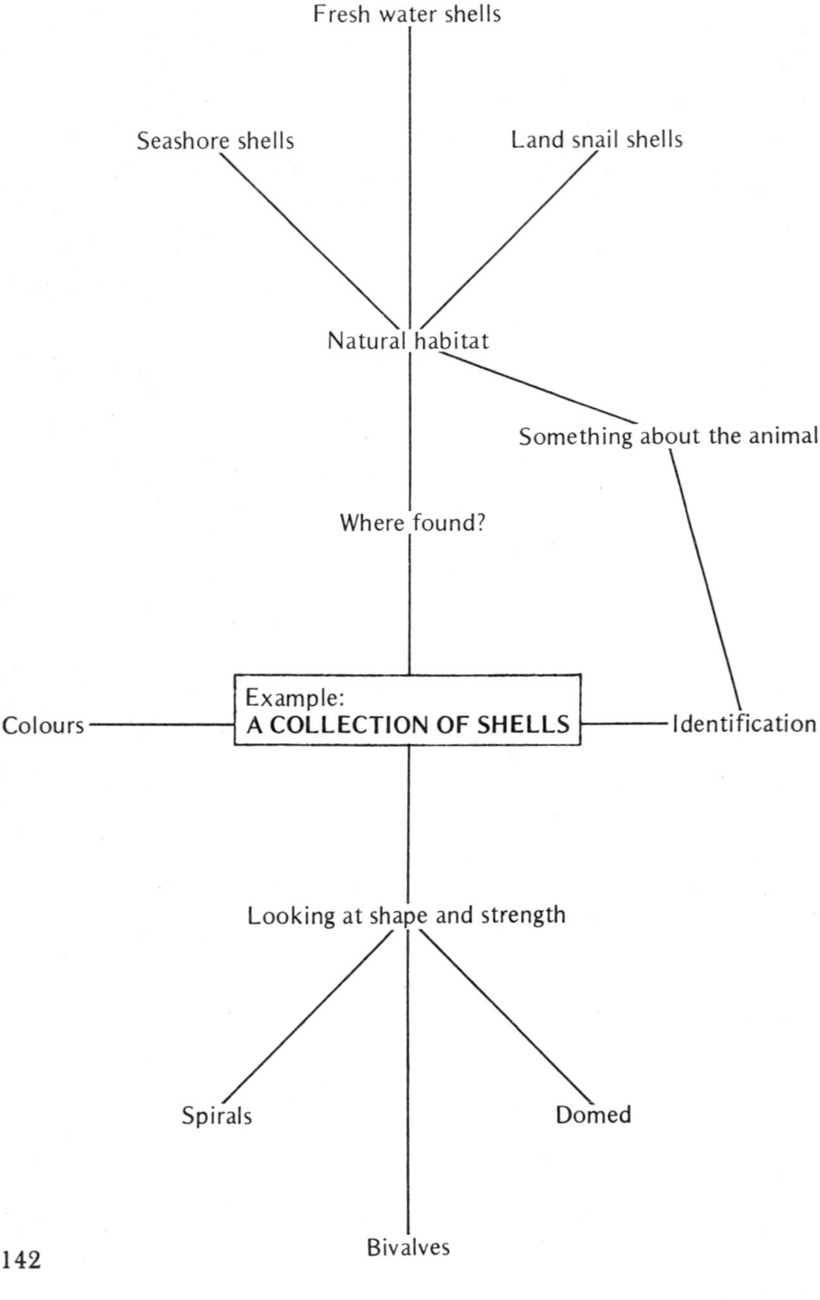

Young children will almost certainly have been doing sorting and grouping in their mathematics lessons, and working with their own collections will entail a considerable amount of work that involves sorting into sets. If the children have, say, a collection of pebbles picked up at random off a beach they can decide for themselves how these pebbles are to be grouped. They may want to split them into 'big ones' and 'little ones' but they may be able to use more sophisticated criteria and divide according to markings, colour, weight or shape. It is largely immaterial; they have made the effort to gather together a collection, and they are now using it as the basis for further work.

The display of collections should be treated seriously and the children given enough room to work and to show their collections. They should also be taught to look after these displays for themselves — particularly if it necessitates watering plants etc. Displays should also be changed frequently. Nothing is more boring than looking at the same theme day after day, and constant change ensures that the children are always on the look out for something new and exciting.

Any school will, of course, want to display children's work as well as possible, but children tend to regard things they have collected as very much their personal property and they should be allowed to suggest how the things should be displayed, and to help with the arrangement.

Work from collections can be:

a Directly connected — identifying, labelling, discussing, drawing etc.

b Follow-up work — e.g. having made a collection of different packaging materials the children can devise simple experiments to test the strength of these.

c Investigations — simple work cards can be made, based on the items in the collection, which ask the children to find out something for themselves. For example, a collection of pressed leaves or leaf rubbings could suggest questions such as: 'Which leaf covers the greatest area?' 'Which leaves are made up of smaller leaflets?' etc.

GENERAL NOTES

1 Displaying collections

a Some items are best displayed in boxes. Small boxes covered in cellophane are useful, and matchbox trays can be glued onto a strong piece of card to produce a display panel made up of small compartments. Collect gift boxes with cellophane lids or made entirely of cellophane, and small, clear glass jars. Shoe boxes are useful for larger items, and if one side is cut away the inside can be painted to make a suitable setting for the specimens. For example, a shoe box painted blue on the sides, and with sand stuck on the bottom with a glue such as Dufix, could be used to display shells, dried seaweed etc.

b A pond-life collection will need a tank of some sort. Use the largest you can (but remember that once it is filled with water it will be extremely heavy), but if the orthodox kind is not available use a plastic washing-up bowl or an old sink, or plastic sweet jars. The latter are easily obtainable and if the tops are cut off they are quite strong, although rather small. Cover the bottom with a layer of grit or washed sand, and put in a few stones. Pond weed can be anchored down with the stones, or can be planted in small pots of soil, with stones on the top to prevent the mud seeping out. When filling the tank put a sheet of stiff paper on the bottom and pour the water onto this to prevent disturbing the sand and weed. Try and leave the tank standing for three or four days before putting any animals into it, and as the idea is to try and imitate the natural environment as far as possible add some pond water and some of the pond's bottom mud (to provide food in the form of water fleas, diatoms etc).

c Cages for Spiders, caterpillars and other small animals will be needed (see Sections 8 and 9).

d Provide children with card to mount flat specimens — pressed flowers and leaves, grasses, leaf and bark rubbings, samples of paper, yarns, fabrics etc.

2 The children can use the tape recorder to make commentaries to go with their specimens. These can be used with small tape recorders and left with the displays for other children to hear, e.g.

> This is a collection of bones. All of these bones came from birds or mammals and were found by children in our class. Number 1 is a bird's skull. You can see the beak and the holes where the eyes were. Number 2 is from a Sheep. It is one of the bones from the spine. Numbers 3, 4 and 5 are Rabbit bones. We think that they are all leg bones.

The collection and tape recording can be reinforced by slides and a small viewer. For example, with the above recording, slides of a rabbit, a sheep and a bird could be shown.

WORKING AND RECORDING

1 Once the children have gathered their collection together they will need to set about identifying and labelling. The youngest children will not be able to do this without help but they should tell you what they want written. Labelling can be very simple, e.g.

> These are flowers we found round the school field.
> Class 1 have collected all these pieces of paper.
> Children in this class brought these shells back from their holidays.

Or it can be more detailed showing evidence of identification, e.g.

We made rubbings of leaves. (The leaf rubbings are then mounted and labelled – Oak, Ash, Plane, Sycamore etc.)

In this tank are all the things we found at Spencer's Pond. (A list can then be made of the specimens found, or a separate label can be made for each one with the name and a picture. These labels can be stuck on the tank or on a separate chart.)

Tape recordings can be made, as explained above.

2 Identification will not be easy with many of the things collected by children but where this is impractical the specimens should be grouped in some way, e.g.

a *A collection of yarns* Possible groupings — yarns used for knitting, thick yarns, thin yarns, yarns made by twisting several threads together (plied), red (blue, brown, green, yellow etc) yarns, threads pulled out of pieces of material, threads used for sewing, smooth yarns, hairy yarns.

b *A collection of shells* Possible groupings — spiral shells, flat shells, domed shells, shells in two parts (bivalves), small shells, large shells, black and grey shells, coloured shells.

c *A collection of stones* Possible groupings — stones found on the shore (in the garden, park etc), smooth stones, rough stones, stones with holes in them, brightly coloured stones, stones used for building, polished stones.

3 Work arising from the collections will vary. With the younger children sorting and discussing will probably be sufficient but the older children should ask questions about the things they have found, and should be able to think of ways of answering these questions. Here are some examples of follow-up work:

a Leaves — assessment of area and perimeter; looking at damage to leaves caused by caterpillars etc.

b Garden weeds — graphs showing the commonest; a look at the ways in which the plants spread; ways of getting rid of weeds in a garden.

c Fruits and seeds — ways of dispersal; experiments to find out how far a dandelion 'parachute' will travel; fruits and seeds eaten by animals or birds.

d Shells — looking at spiral shells and other spirals (climbing plants, tendrils etc); testing strength of, say, a limpet shell. A piece of wood can be placed over the top and children can stand on this. Is the shell easy to break? Why does it need to be strong? Study of snails.

e Food plants — how are they eaten? Ways of cooking food plants; a look at other useful plants; grouping them according to how they grow (under ground, in pods, leafy plants etc).

f Yarns — finding the composition of yarns by unravelling them; testing strength by hanging weights (or arbitrary weights) on them to find the breaking point; simple card weaving; twisting and spinning wool with a simple spindle. This can be made with a piece of dowel and a circle of wood drilled in the centre to push the dowel through. If possible let the children collect sheep's wool off hedges and fences.

g Packaging — testing the strength of boxes; finding out if packages are damp proof; finding out how easy it is to open a package.

h Postage stamps with, say, animals on them — finding out about each animal from books; making a card index of the animals. Each card can have the name, habitat and some information on it.

i Tools — demonstration of the tools being used. These can be the tools related to a particular craft, and it may be possible to get parents to help with this, e.g. woodworking tools — hammer, plane, saw, hand-drill, screwdriver, chisel.

j Bones — looking at the shapes; looking at a long bone to see the hollow shaft and finding out why bones should be hollow (older children could devise some tests for comparing the strengths of tubes); talking about ancient people and the fact that they used bones as tools; making a 'needle' from a piece of bone; finding out more about skeletons — structure, movement between bones, protection of organs.

WORKING AND RECORDING

Any work done based on a collection should be included with the display of the items, or the children concerned can explain to other groups what they have done, why and what they have found out. If they have developed a simple piece of apparatus they can show how they made it and how it works.

Question cards, work cards and work sheets can be made to help with any additional work. Some children will be able to supply the questions for these themselves.

Flowers

What is the commonest colour of the flowers collected?

How could you find out if insects like to visit flowers of this colour?

Paper

For some of this work you will need some paper bags. Try and get about 10 different ones.

1 How many different samples of paper have you found?
2 Can you sort these into groups showing the way they are used?
e.g.
paper for writing on
paper for printing on
paper for wrapping food
paper to put on walls
other papers.
3 Can you think of a way of finding out which of the paper bags is the strongest?

This work sheet is based on a collection of living things found in the school grounds.

School collection **Name** ....

1 Which of these did you find?

Woodlouse	☐	Earwig	☐
Ladybird	☐	Other beetle	☐
Earthworm	☐	Snail	☐
Housefly	☐	Wasp	☐
Bee	☐	Butterfly	☐
Greenfly	☐	Caterpillar	☐

Anything else ....

2 Which of these flowers did you find?

Daisy	☐	Buttercup	☐	Dandelion	☐
Groundsel	☐	Willow Herb	☐	Shepherd's Purse	☐
Chickweed	☐	Dead nettle	☐	Stinging nettle	☐

Any others ....

3 How many sorts of grasses did you find? ....

4 Are there any trees? ....

How many? ....

5 Did you ever see any of these?

Birds .... Cats ....

Obviously this type of work sheet can be varied to include the particular items in which the children are most interested.

SUPPORT MATERIAL

Books for the children

Books listed on pages 140-141.
Books about the particular items collected by the children.

Books for teacher reference

Books listed on page 141.
Display and Presentation in Schools Christopher Jarman (A. and C. Black)
Wildlife Conservation by Young People Neil Arnold (Ward Lock Educational)

Useful apparatus

Shoe boxes; matchboxes etc for making display trays; clear cellophane; card and felt pens for notices; cassette tape recorders; slide viewer; small glass jars; strong adhesive; containers for water collections; display space — tables and boards; small weights or washers; string; scissors; Sellotape.

24 TRAILS

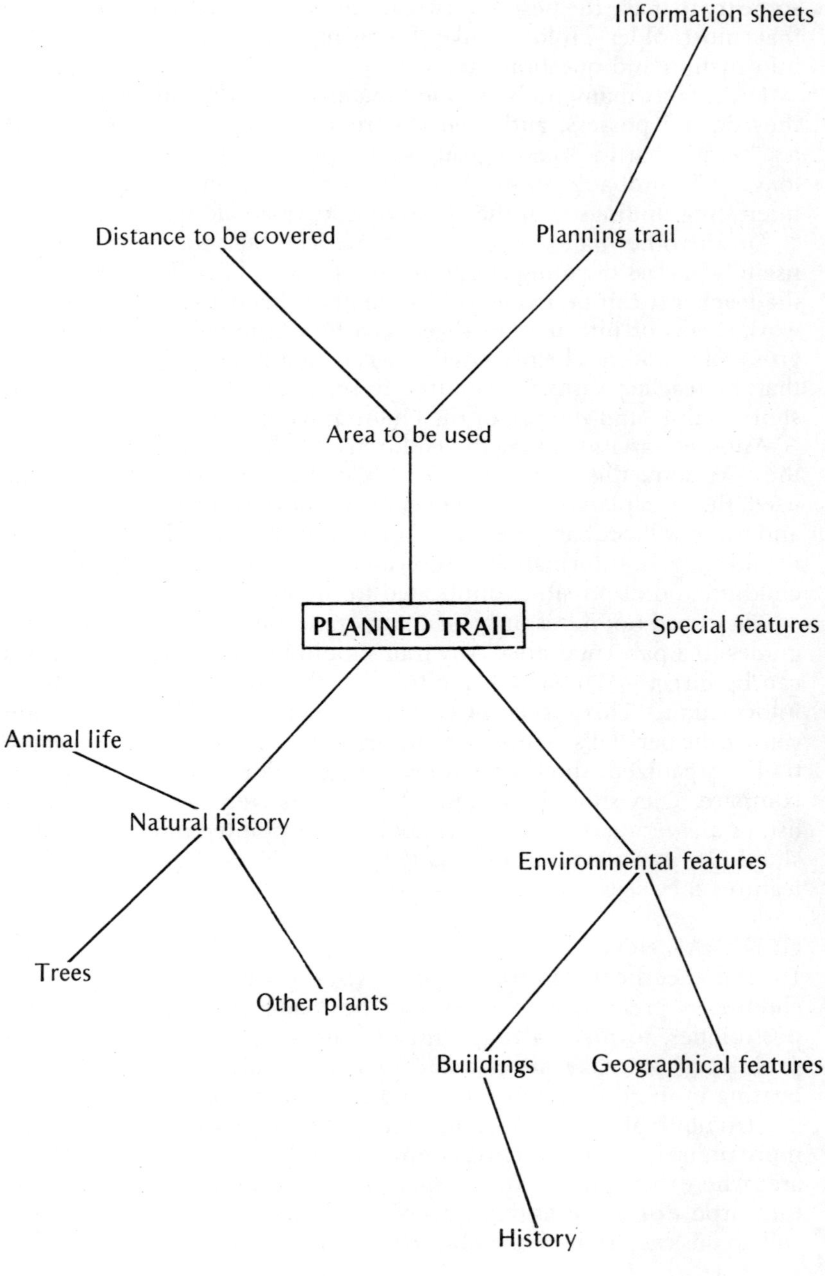
Information sheets
Distance to be covered
Planning trail
Area to be used
PLANNED TRAIL
Special features
Animal life
Natural history
Environmental features
Trees
Other plants
Buildings
Geographical features
History

Nature trails in National Trust forests and reserves, in parks and in the grounds of stately homes are familiar to all of us. Many are of considerable value, pointing out things that people might well miss; some try to make the best of very scant resources, but there is no doubt that most older children like following them, armed with their information and question sheets.

For infants many trails are too long and require reading skills that they do not possess, and even if parts are carefully selected by the teacher it is hard to keep a group of five or six year olds interested for long. It is probably more practical to ramble, and to discuss any interesting findings with the children as they go along.

On the other hand, an organized trail can be a way of occupying, usefully, a class of young children, and if the trail has been devised by the teacher it can be made to include items likely to appeal, and any work sheets or information sheets can be put together for a specific group of children. The prepared trail can incorporate all those features that the teacher wants the children to see, and it can be as long or as short as time and the age of the children will allow.

Another variation is for the children to help prepare the trail, and they like doing this. If they are taken, first of all, to look at the area to be used, they can plan routes and decide on features worth pointing out – and these will probably be quite different from those that the teacher would suggest. Information sheets can be written and illustrated by the children and, if possible, duplicated for other children to use.

They need not necessarily be nature trails, but they should be mini-guides to a particular area. Any trail should be informative and notes can be direct – 'This is a Plane tree', or they can provide additional information – 'This is a Plane tree. Plane trees grow well in towns. As you can see the bark falls off the trunk in large pieces.' The aim, however the trail is organized, should be to encourage children to observe and to compare. They should not wander about passively ticking items off a list, or answering dull questions about items pointed out to them, but should be stimulated into thinking for themselves about some of the features they see.

GENERAL NOTES

1 Whether the trail is to be organized by the teacher alone or with the children a preliminary visit should be made to the area to assess possibilities, to make a rough list of features and, if the area seems promising, to make an estimate of a reasonable walking distance bearing in mind the age of the children concerned.

2 Do not look only at obvious 'trail' places but consider some of the more unlikely ones too. This is important if the school is situated in an area where there are few, or no, open or wild places. Whilst a trail can be the purpose of an outing (e.g. a zoo visit), it has to be remembered that it will, in this case, only be possible to visit once and so the only follow-up

will have to be in the classroom. If children are helping, the trail needs to be somewhere they can visit easily, and where other groups can go and try it out. Some examples of possible trails are:

a *Woodland, moorland, field and shore trails* Here the only difficulty should be in selecting the best and most interesting area.
b *A garden trail* Possible if a parent or teacher is willing to let you use theirs!
c *A park trail* This can vary from a formally laid-out park to a virtually wild one. Obviously the latter is the best for children but any park will contain some features that can be used.
d *School grounds trail* This can be set up wherever the school is situated. Even the most unlikely area with nothing but an asphalted yard has something to offer – the buildings, their history, a wall, plants growing from cracks and gutters, Woodlice, Earwigs, Houseflies, Moss, Lichens, visiting birds, domestic cats etc.
e *A street trail* Small children will need adequate supervision if they are to look at things in streets, but there are so many things to see that it is worth arranging. On the preliminary visit look for trees, gardens, waste land, weeds, bridges, churches and church yards, street signs, other street furniture, shops, roof features, old buildings, road names, doors and windows and open spaces. This type of trail can be used to study the history, geography and natural history of the local environment.
f *Roadside or hedge trail*
g *Waste-land trail*
h *Specialized trails such as farm or zoo trails.*

3 Make use of the public library. It may contain a local studies section and a great deal of information can be found there about the immediate area. It is particularly interesting, in towns, to find the origin of the street names. For example, why is a grubby street, squashed between factories, called Green Lane or Cherry Orchard? Local museums, too, are valuable sources of information and are worth a visit to see which exhibits could be of use to the children.
4 Information books will be needed for this work and it is worth being prepared by having them ready for use. Some of these could even be books made by a previous class, e.g. a book of pressed, labelled leaves would make a useful reference book for other children to use.
5 Basically a trail is a route punctuated by items of interest, and in devising one it is necessary to make sure that the children concerned will be able to see these easily. Also, some rules are always necessary:

Never go onto other people's property without permission.
Always shut gates behind you.
Do not drop litter.
Never frighten animals in any way.
Do not damage plants.

WORKING AND RECORDING

Preparing or walking the trail will be the major part of this work. The youngest infants can be told beforehand what to expect and can discuss the items of interest as they go. Back in the classroom they can draw the things they have seen and these can be mounted to make a 'trail frieze'.

The children who are reading can fill in their question sheets and augment these with pictures and models back in the classroom. If they are preparing a trail the information sheets themselves will constitute the recording of work done.

Examples of trail information sheets

1 Teacher-produced trail, using a small local park, and although the children will look around generally, the main aim is to look at the trees there.

Park Trail Name . . . .

1 We will go into the park through the big gates. These are large gates made of metal. The name of the man who made them is on one of the gates.

What is his name? . . . .

What can you see on the top of the gates? . . . .

Why do you think these have been put there? . . . .

2 Turn left when you go through the gates and walk up the path. The trees by the path are Lime trees.

How many can you see? . . . .

Can you draw a Lime leaf here:

3 At the end of the path look at the area in front of you. Which of these can you see?

a pond	a tall chimney	a bridge	a railway line
a church	a road	an old wall	a canal

4 Look at the wall.

What is it made of? . . . .

Are there any plants growing on it? . . . .

Can you name any of them? . . . .

Do you think this is an old or new wall? . . . .

How do you know? . . . .

5 Now go onto the grass area.

What can you see all round the grass? ....
Have you seen any birds? ....
There are lots of trees here. You can make rubbings of the leaves and bark. We can find out the names when we get back to school.

2 Children-suggested trail using the local churchyard (of an old church in a country town). Obviously the children should be told where they can walk, and what they can do.

St Anne's Churchyard Trail

This is an old churchyard and people are not buried here any more. Some of the stones are very old, and a lot of them are not looked after any more. There are a lot of weeds in the churchyard. These are some questions for you to find out. You can get the answers off Class 2b when you get back to school.

The tree by the gate is very poisonous for animals. What is its name? ....
What is the oldest date you can find on the gravestones? .....
What is the name on this stone? ....
Write down ten ladies' names (Christian/first names) from the stones:

....
....
....
....
....

What is the picture carved on the gravestone of Joseph Walton? ....
What has happened to the stones under the chestnut tree? Why can't you read them any more? ....
How many weeds can you find in the grass? If you don't know the names, take one with you and look it up when you get back to school. ....
There is a stone which says Mary Jane Borrowdale. It gives the names of her children. How many did she have? ....
What were the boys' names? ....
....

What did John Borrowdale do? . . . .
The wall round the churchyard is old too. Write down how you know this. . . . .
. . . .
. . . .

3 Planned trail for very young children in school grounds (with a playground, a small garden area, and a small field with a fence round it and two small Horse Chestnut trees).

Teacher's notes for school trail Points for discussion are marked*
1 Go out of rear door and start at the corner of the field by the gate. This gate has not been used for a long time and is overgrown with weeds and a Blackberry plant.*
2 Walk along by the fence. You can see Convolvulus* in spring and summer. This is twined round the fence. Look at the way it climbs.
3 Just past this the fence has a hole in it. Something obviously comes through here because of the track* (not big enough for a child). Get children to suggest what.
4 Plants* growing round the field are mostly Grass, Dandelion, Buttercup, Groundsel, Plantain and there is a patch of Vetch in one corner.
5 At the end of the field there are three Horse Chestnut trees*. They are all fairly small and have not flowered yet. Look at leaves*, buds*, and bark*. One tree is very scratched (?cats)*. Look at the green alga on the trunks*.
6 Along the third side of the field is a track* made by children regularly walking along there to get to the playground (having come through a gap in the fence). Discuss tracks and pathways.
7 The wall* at the front of the playground is part of the original school wall. Possibly built about 1890. Look at the brick patterns*, Moss* and Ragwort growing along the top*.
8 Cross playground to garden. This is planted with Roses. Look at thorns*. Usually there are a number of weeds* here. Collect samples for display in classroom.

Collect leaves, grasses etc as we go round. Make these into display, and make frieze later.
Other things we may see — Cats*, Starlings* (and other birds), Dogs*, insects* and Snails* (often found on the fence by the gate).

SUPPORT MATERIAL

Books for the children

The Seashore and Seashore Life Nancy Scott (Ladybird Books)

Exploring the Park Leslie Jackman (Evans)
Exploring the Hedgerow Leslie Jackman (Evans)
Exploring the Garden Leslie Jackman (Evans)
Exploring the Woodland Leslie Jackman (Evans)
Plants B. J. Bampton (Macmillan)
Along a Road Philip Sauvain (Macmillan)
In a Garden Philip Sauvain (Macmillan)

Books for teacher reference
Learning from Trails R. W. Colton and R. F. Morgan (Longman for the Schools Council)
Looking Around in Town and Country Philip Sauvain (Franklin Watts)
The Ecology of Woodlands Alfred Leutscher (Franklin Watts)
Know Your Conifers (Forestry Commission Booklet 15) Herbert L. Edlin (HMSO)
Canals C. Vialls (A. and C. Black)
School Projects in Natural History Devon Trust for Nature Conservation (Heinemann)
What on Earth Are We Doing? D. H. Keen and G. E. Simmons (Ladybird Books)

Useful apparatus
Clip boards made from hardboard or very strong card with a bulldog clip; attach a pencil to each of these with a piece of string.

25 OURSELVES

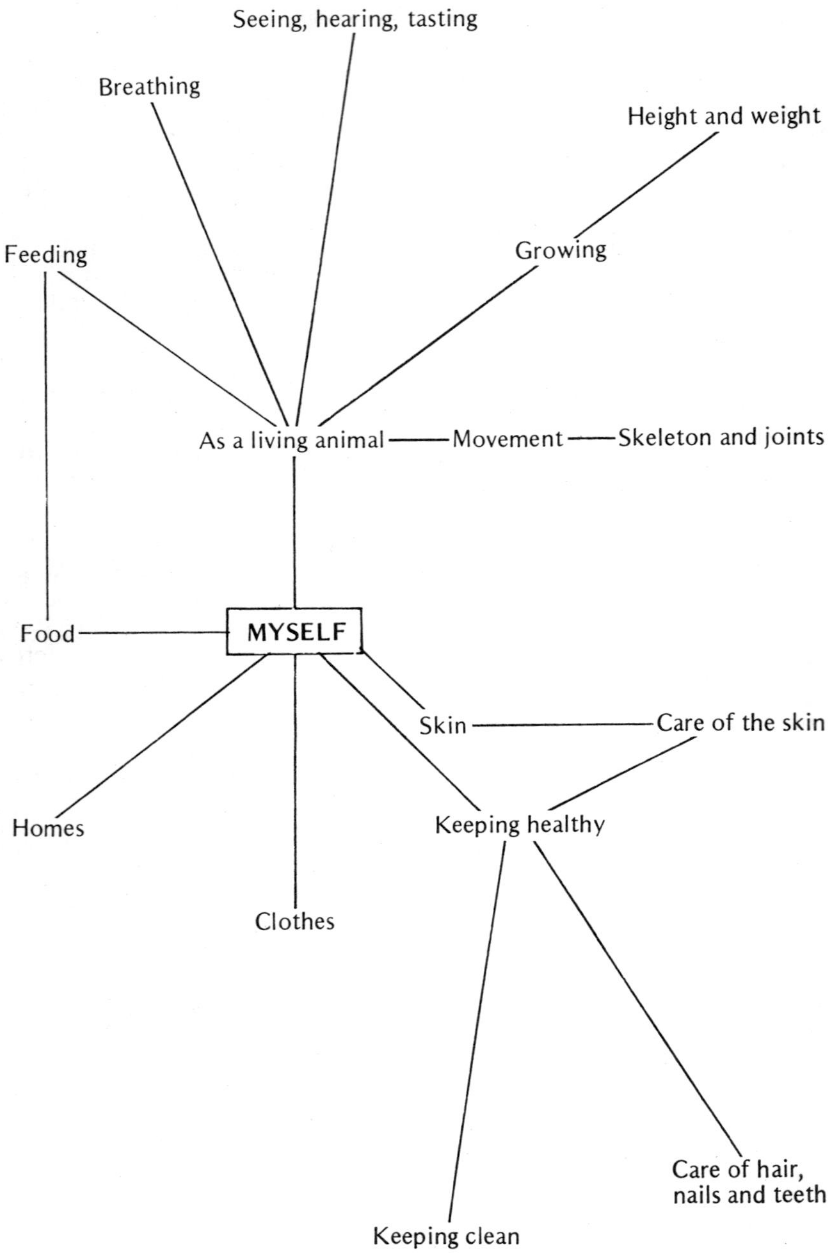

Children know what they look like. They know that they have two arms, two legs, two eyes, two ears and a nose! They know that their hair and nails grow and have to be cut, and they know that they can move from place to place by using their legs. If they cut or scratch themselves they bleed, but will heal reasonably rapidly. They will also realize that they have to eat and drink, and connect this vaguely with growing and staying alive. Some older children will mention that they need food 'for energy', but this will be information that they have acquired without understanding what it means. (Indeed many adults would find it difficult to explain what is meant by energy.)

'Looking at ourselves' is a useful topic for infant science, and it can be used to introduce young children to some of the important, basic biological concepts. Through this they can learn something about the characteristics of living things, the features of mammals and some elementary health education. All these are topics that they will be studying in greater detail at a later stage and this initial work can be invaluable.

Mathematics is far more interesting if it involves weighing, measuring, and estimating, and children can use the study of themselves for many mathematical investigations. With so many possible subjects available in any classroom, comparison is possible and the children can see the implications of shorter, taller, bigger, smaller etc.

Children are interested in their own bodies but even the older ones often know very little about them. Very few of them realize that they are animals, belonging to the group known as the mammals, and are often very amused to find that they have something in common with cows, mice and hedgehogs!

Any study undertaken should aim at making the children look at living things in general, and themselves in particular, in the hope that they will begin to understand something about their own anatomy and physiology, and the need to care for their bodies.

GENERAL NOTES

1 Man is a mammal and therefore warm blooded and vertebrate, but is unlike other mammals in that he has assumed an erect position for moving about. Man's skeleton is made up of 206 bones of different shapes and sizes. The largest is the femur (thigh bone) and the smallest are the three tiny bones in the ear (the ossicles).

2 Like other living things, mammals reproduce, feed, breathe, grow, move, excrete and react to stimuli. Growth is very fast between birth and six months old, and again in the early teens. The head stops growing before the rest of the body, and is virtually full size by the age of ten. Once full height is reached (between eighteen and twenty years) a person will not grow any taller, but he may grow fatter and heavier.

3 The surface of the body is covered with skin. This skin helps to

regulate temperature and protects the body from water, harmful substances and bacteria. The colour of the skin depends on the pigment in it, and skin colour among humans varies very considerably.

4 Mathematically parts of the body were used for measurement long before standard measures were introduced. The obvious disadvantages of this can be seen if these arbitrary measures are tested. (It must have been far better to buy a 'yard' of cloth from a tall man with long arms than from someone with very short arms!)

A fathom — the length of rope held between the hands with the arms stretched out sideways (standard measure — 6 feet).
A foot — the length of a man's foot (12 inches).
A hand — the width of the hand at the base of the fingers (4 inches).
A cubit — the length from elbow to finger tips (this is an old measure and was about 18 to 22 inches).
A yard — the length from the tip of the nose to the finger tips of one arm stretched out sideways (3 feet; 36 inches).
An inch — probably the width of the thumb.
A span — length between the tip of the thumb and the tip of the little finger with the fingers outstretched (9 inches).

5 Any study of 'ourselves' will include basic health education:

care of skin, nails, hair, teeth and feet
eyes and ears
clothing, homes and food

PLANNING AND PREPARATION

If children are going to make a study of themselves it is useful to look at all the possibilities, and to select topics suitable to each particular age group.

1 **Living things**

Young children can look at any animals available and see if they do all the things characteristic of living organisms.

Do they move about in any way?
Do they feed? What do they feed on? Can you see them feeding?
Do they breathe? Can you see an animal breathing? How do you know it is breathing?
Do they grow?
Do they reproduce? What are the baby animals like? Do they look like the parents?
Do they get rid of waste?
Do they react in any way to outside stimuli (being touched, jumping at loud noises etc)?

When the children have looked at animals they can decide if humans do the same things. It is useful to collect as many pictures of animals as possible, and to make arrangements for the children to see living animals — domestic animals, farm animals, zoo animals and small pets.

2 **Bones and skeletons**

Children seem to like bones and skeletons. They can look at any bones you have been able to collect and can decide if they have skeletons. They can look at another child moving about, and can see where the moving joints are, and they can look at their own hands.

3 **Measuring**

a They can use parts of the body for measuring.
b They can make measurements of themselves and other children. The older children can measure height and weight reasonably accurately using a height-measure and personal scales. Younger children can measure height on a chart pinned on the wall, and can compare heights of children in the class.

4 **Growth**

If pets are kept in school children can see that the baby animals grow fairly rapidly. For example, the baby Guinea Pigs are much smaller than the adults, but soon grow to full size. It may be possible to arrange for a mother to bring her baby to school and show him or her to the children. They know that babies grow into children and then into adults, but when they see a real baby they can more readily understand that they are not only bigger, but they are able to do things that the baby cannot do. Their own growth is not obvious except over a length of time but they can keep height measures which are checked once or twice each term over the year.

5 **Eyes**

Collect pictures of eyes and devise some experiments to teach the children something about sight:

a Wrap up some parcels. Ask the children what is inside them. They can guess the contents, but can only be certain if they actually see what is inside.
b Ask them to write or draw with their eyes covered. Is it easier with the eyes open?
c Stand the children in a circle except for one child in the middle. He should have his eyes covered. He is asked to touch a particular child. Can he do this without seeing?
d Ask children simple questions about a familiar object while their eyes are covered, e.g.
This is my coat. What colour is it?
Has it got any buttons?
Has it got any pockets?
How many pockets has it got?
What is there on the collar of my coat?
Are there any buttons on the sleeves?

Ask them to look and answer the questions again.

Talk about spectacles (have several pairs to show them). Decide why some people wear these and stress how nice people look in them. There are still some children who will not readily accept wearing glasses.

6 Ears

Look at pictures of the ears of animals. Look at our ears. Prepare a tape of familiar sounds for the children to listen to and identify. Keep the sounds to those likely to be familiar to the children, but include one or two harder ones to provoke discussion, e.g. dog barking, pouring water, scrubbing, banging a drum, scratching, clapping, crumpling paper, dropping a plate (and breaking it), whistling, snoring, tearing cloth etc.

7 Hair

Older children can experiment to find the strength of a hair. Attach a long hair to a stand with sticky tape, and tape a loop of paper to the other end. Nails can be put into the paper loop until the hair breaks. Do all hairs break with the same number of nails in the paper?

8 Skin and sensitivity

Children can experiment to see if they can distinguish between warm and cold objects, and various 'feel' boxes can be devised. Using a large shoe box cut a hole in one end, large enough for a child to put his hand through. Cut a piece of cloth big enough to cover the hole and tape it, along the top only, on the inside of the box so that it covers the hole. The child can then push his hand inside without being able to see into the hole. Put different objects inside and ask the children to distinguish these by touch only. Small objects can be put inside cloth bags and the children can feel these. Texture cards can be made for feeling — sandpaper, velvet, plastic, cloth, paper etc.

WORKING AND RECORDING

The work that can be done is so extensive that suggestions can only be indications of possible topics.

The youngest children can look at animals for specific reasons, e.g. to

see how they move
look at their eyes or ears
find out what sort of food they eat
look at baby animals.

They can make zig-zag books showing these, and including themselves, as examples.

A large outline shape of a child can be labelled to show parts of the body (even if the children are still unable to read). These should be accurate, even if simplified, and the parts indicated should be seen on a child before labelling the diagram. The same type of diagram could be used for marking in the position of joints after the children have looked at ways of moving.

Joints in the hands can be easily seen and children can see that they can turn their hands over. They will realize the importance of this if they try to pick things up while keeping the palms downwards. Stiff paper mittens can be made and taped onto a child. He can be asked to carry out simple movements – picking up a pencil, putting on his coat, using a paint brush etc – and will find how difficult this is without the use of the fingers.

The children can collect a list of movement words (having demonstrated each movement to the group):

run	walk	hop	crawl
jump	bend	stretch	climb
step	dance	creep	wriggle
nod	clap	shake	swim

Sizes of hands and feet can be compared by drawing round these to get outlines. Older children can draw these on squared paper and so make a more accurate estimation. Height can be measured against a board with each child's height indicated and labelled with his name. A height graph can be made by measuring each child with a piece of string. Each child can then stick his string onto a large chart.

Older children can use body measurements and can try and find out why these are not very good ways of measuring, e.g. how many feet (i.e. their own feet) long is the classroom? If John does this is it still the same number of feet?

Problem cards can be made so that they can work on their own.

> A span is about 9 inches.
> Check the spans of 10 children and 10 adults.
> Who has a span of 9 inches?

> Who is the tallest girl in the class?
> Who is the tallest boy?
> Who is the shortest girl?
> Which teacher is the tallest?

If they can measure accurately they could also be asked the actual heights.

> Find out who has the biggest hand in the class.
> How will you do this?

Get a very large sheet of paper.
Ask your friend to lie on this, and draw all round him with chalk.
Cut out this outline. Cut out another of the same size.
This will give you some idea of how much skin he has got covering his body.

It is said that a person's height is the same as the measurement between his finger tips with the arms stretched out sideways.

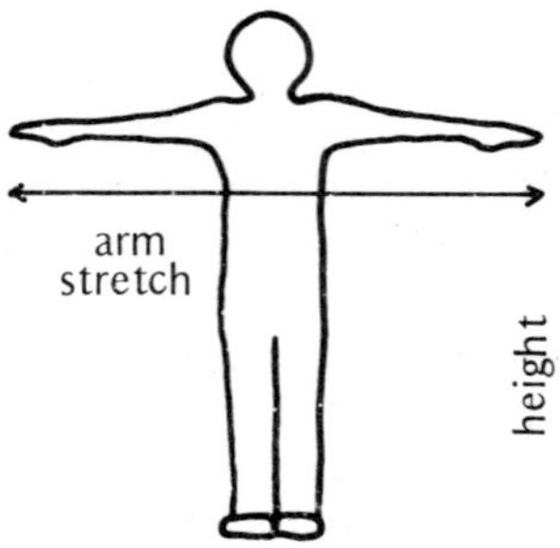

Is this true?

Graphs of hair and eye colouring can be made and the children can set questions which can be answered using the graphs, e.g.

How many children in the class have black hair?
Are there any children with red hair?
How many fair-haired boys are there?

Work about food can be varied according to age. The five year olds can collect pictures of food from magazines and can divide these into sets, e.g.

milk foods	fruits	vegetables
foods made from flour	meats	things you drink

They can taste some foods and find out the meanings of sweet and sour. Older children can look at some foods and can make large charts to show different foods e.g.

Milk and things made from milk
Vegetables
Meat and fish
Things we like to eat
Flour, and things made from flour.

Health education can begin very early. It starts as soon as the child is taught that he should wash his hands before eating or after using the lavatory. 'Keeping clean' can be a topic for young children and this can include washing ourselves, washing our clothes, looking after hair and nails, soap, water etc. The care of teeth and feet are both important and can be introduced. The older infants could make simple posters:

Wash your hands before dinner.
Have you cleaned your teeth today?
These are good for you (pictures of foods).

Health education work lends itself to displays, friezes, class books and demonstrations, and the children can be involved in all of these. There are so many possibilities that they will probably think of many more topics for themselves, and they may be able to organize a class or school exhibition on a specific subject, e.g. A 'Clean Hands' Week.

One reception class made outlines of every child in the class — full size — and coloured in hair and eyes and each child then 'dressed' his own outline in clothes he had made from paper. Obviously they needed a great deal of help but the results were not only colourful and attractive but the children had learnt the very basic facts that they had arms, legs, ears, eyes, noses, mouths etc and that they varied in size, hair and skin colouring and types of dress.

SUPPORT MATERIAL

Books for the children

Looking at Me Romola Showell (Ward Lock Educational)
Seeing Kate Miller (OUP)
Hearing Kate Miller (OUP)
The Book about Me Birgit Ginnerup (Methuen)
Your Skin and Mine Paul Showers (A. & C. Black)
Look at Your Eyes Paul Showers (A. & C. Black)
Touch and Feel K. A. Shoesmith (Burke Books)
Things to Hear Henry Pluckrose (Franklin Watts)
Taste and Flavour K. A. Shoesmith (Burke Books)

Books for teacher reference

Ourselves Science 5/13 (Macdonald Educational)
Introduction to Biology D. G. Mackean (John Murray)

Useful apparatus

Height measure; personal scales; string; old magazines for pictures of foods and clothes etc; tape recorder; shoe boxes; squared paper.

26 EXPLORING AND DISCOVERING

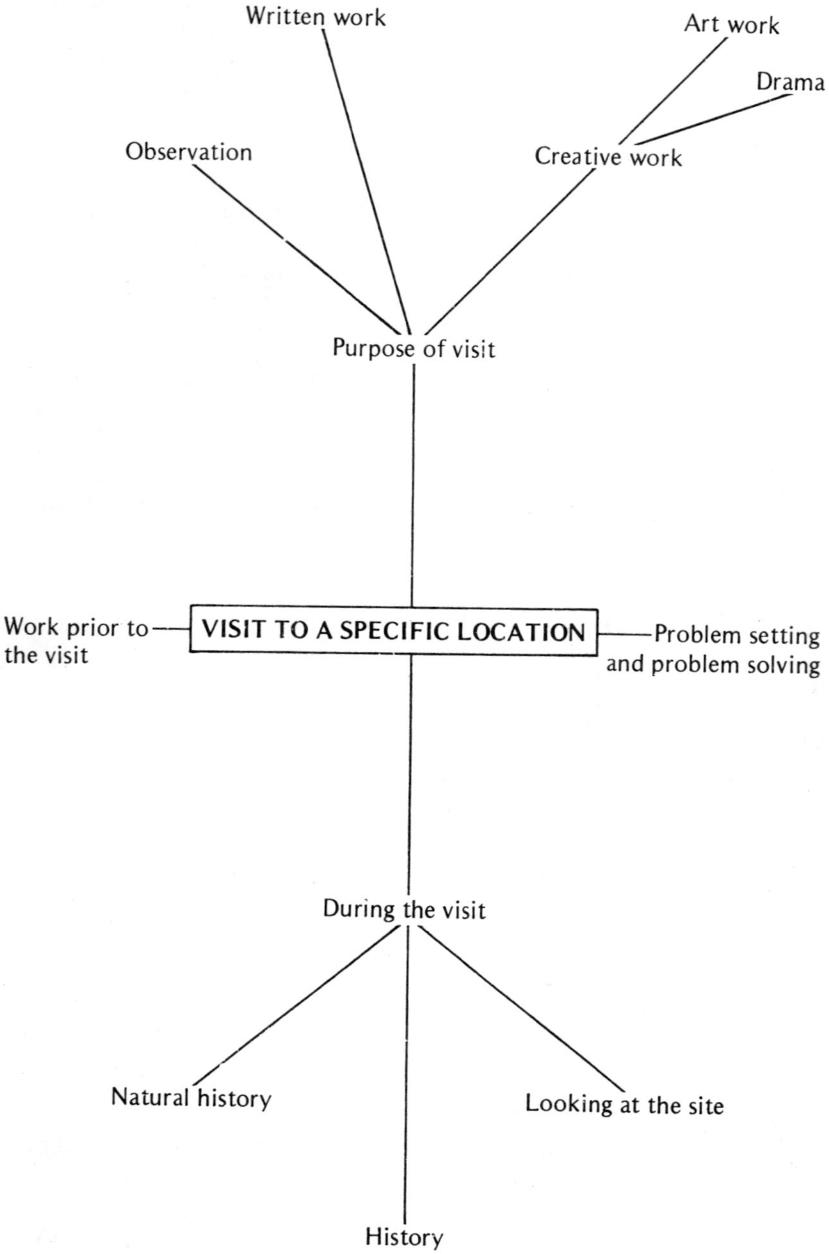

Children respond to, and learn from, their surroundings and should be given opportunities to explore beyond the classroom. There cannot be a set list of things that they should see and do — so much depends on the environment and the needs of the children — but their curiosity about their immediate world can be exploited and used to their benefit.

Any project which gives them the chance to make discoveries for themselves must be planned to suit individual needs, and should aim to sharpen their perception and give them practice in thinking about their surroundings in terms of space, size and number. As they get older their attention can be concentrated on particular objects or themes which interest them.

Letting children explore sounds relatively easy if it is assumed that, turned loose, they will seek out things for themselves, but this is so rarely the case that considerable planning is needed if children are to work purposefully and gain experience in carrying out simple investigations.

Rules for exploring the immediate environment cannot be laid down; in the country there are so many possibilities that a careful selection has to be made; in the town the planning may involve finding out about the material available.

Visits can be a pleasure or a nightmare, but I feel that there should be a definite reason for any visit. This may well be a social reason, but it can also be the stepping-off point for a particular study, or the opportunity to see and learn about something outside the children's normal sphere.

> One of the first questions asked by many teachers wishing to make more use of the outdoor environment is 'How shall we begin?' The most obvious suggestion children and teachers can agree to follow is 'Let's go and see what's there'; for some general looking and probing around is necessary if children are to have opportunities of discovering what really is there and so be in a position to choose their own investigations.
>
> *Using the Environment — Early Explorations* (Science 5/13)

GENERAL NOTES

1 One of the first things that children need to be taught is how to look! If asked to look at a house and to describe it they will probably mention doors, windows and chimneys and any outstanding features such as ivy growing all over the walls and bright red curtains, but they will be unlikely to mention that the brickwork is old and showing signs of deterioration, that sparrows are nesting under the eaves or that the chimney pots are an unusual shape.

2 Features which children can be encouraged to look at will vary according to the position of the school but they can include:

buildings in general

particular features of buildings — doors, windows, roofs, plaques, ornamentation, chimneys, towers etc
street names
street furniture
industrial features
railway lines and canals
village features
farms
walls
fields and crops
animals in captivity or natural habitats
prehistoric sites
local plant and animal life
local geological features
rivers, lakes and ponds
seashores
specific sites — airports, lighthouses, harbours etc.

3 Apparently unimportant features can start a discovery project, e.g.

Prints of dog paws in mud→work on tracks and trails.
Felled trees→work on the age of trees; annual rings; use of wood.
Road being resurfaced→work on road-making materials; smell of tar; pleasant and unpleasant smells.
Willow Herb seeds being blown about→work on seed dispersal; plants growing on waste ground.

4 Many children walk to school every day, and those who don't will have some other walk with which they are so familiar that they will not notice the things they pass. These walks serve as very good starting points for discovery work.

a *Town pavement* How is it made? Is it old or new? Has it a curb? Are there any drains, hydrants, lamps, notices etc?
What are pavements for? Why were they built? How old are they?
b *Footpaths* Have the public right of way? Where does the path go to? Is it used regularly? Who uses it? Has it got a name? Are there any plants around?
If this is a country footpath this will be an opportunity to discuss the Country Code, and point out to children the necessity of shutting gates, keeping to the path, and keeping dogs on leads.
c *Tracks* Has the track been made by animals? Which animals? Why do they use it? Has the track been made by humans? Is it an old or new track?
d *Nature walks and trails* – see Section 24.
e *Special pathways* – bridleways, towpaths, rope walks, alleyways.

If we accept the fact that any journey undertaken on foot is, technically, a walk then this work can lead on to stories about famous journeys:

The ascent of Everest
Scott's journey to the South Pole
Stanley's journey to find Livingstone
The crossing of Australia by Burke and Wills.

PLANNING AND PREPARATION

1 Visits need to be planned and, whenever .possible, the teacher should go beforehand to find out exactly what is available. Details of planning visits, however minor they appear to be, can be found in *'Organizing Schools Journeys'* by Michael Arkinstall, and even if the trip to the local park seems not to merit detailed planning it is useful to be reminded that small children can get lost and adequate supervision and labelling are wise precautions!

2 For younger children an organized visit is an exciting occasion, but nothing is more boring than going back to school and being asked to write or talk about 'the visit'. It is far more useful to let the children enjoy the outing as a whole and to concentrate on one particular aspect for extended work. For example a visit to the zoo is too extensive for children to take in every detail. Back at school they can concentrate on, say:

animal covering
birds
the cat family
animal camouflage

3 Possible visits for young children:

a local zoo
a wild-life park or bird sanctuary
a farm park
a farm
parks and gardens (if there is something there likely to be of interest)
castle and castle ruins
fields, hedgerows, lanes etc
seashore and pond
woodland and moorland
an airport
local craft workshop
fire station, local factory, garage (particularly if there is a parent involved who could help arrange this)
local museum if it houses exhibits likely to interest younger children, e.g. a natural history museum, old vehicles, toys etc.

WORKING AND RECORDING

If the work is to be the result of an organized visit then the children can discuss what they want to do, and can decide for themselves how best to present it. A visit to a farm could include pictures of the animals and some work on the particular animals seen. If the children have seen sheep they can talk about these, their uses to the farmer, shearing, use of wool and the making of woollen cloth. They can try simple spindle spinning and could do some weaving to show the structure of material. All this work can be displayed together with any written or art work.

Class books and murals can include a contribution from every child, and models could be accompanied by taped recordings made at the time of the visit, e.g. animal sounds; talking to a craftsman; interview with the castle curator etc. Work can progress far beyond the visit. For example, a visit to a castle ruin:

Prior to the visit talk about castles and why they were built.
Look at pictures of the buildings and the people who lived in them.
During the visit storming the castle; playing at attacking it; looking at the thickness of the walls; looking at doorways and openings in the walls. Try to see how the people lived; decide why wooden buildings have long since disappeared.
After the visit making models of castles; making pictures; dressing dolls to suit the period; finding stories about castles; making up poems and songs; acting out an attack on a castle; looking at slides of other castles.

If children are going to explore their own environment they can decide on problems they will solve (though, obviously, they are going to need help to formulate these), e.g.

Which plants grow best on waste land?
There is a track across one corner of the field. Who made this? Is it used?
Does all the rubbish thrown down in the park affect the plants growing there?
How many different bushes can we find in the hedge? (see Section 18).
How do some plants manage to grow on walls without soil?
Which children have the most interesting route to school?
Where can we find snails? Which plants do they seem to like best?
There is a large Sycamore tree in the park. How far from the tree are seeds and seedlings found?
What signs of animal feeding can be found in the lane at the side of the churchyard?
Where, along the road, can we find triangular shapes?

The youngest children can be taken to look at one small area, and can make a composite study of this. Back at school they can make a frieze showing all the things they have seen, mount suitable specimens and display interesting things they have found. If the site includes buildings, a camera will be needed.

There is so much work to do and so many possibilities. The materials are all around us. We only need to use our imaginations and a new world is opened up for young children.

SUPPORT MATERIAL

Books for the children

On the Farm Rose Roberts (Nelson)
In the Country Rose Roberts (Nelson)
Let's Look at the Seashore Cathy Kilpatrick (Ward Lock)
Farms Little Learning Library Series (Blackwell)
Exploring the Park Leslie Jackman (Evans)
Exploring the Woodland Leslie Jackman (Evans)
Wild Flowers of Verges and Waste Land Jean Imrie (A. and C. Black)
Castles Starters Series (Macdonald Educational)
Rocks Starters Series (Macdonald Educational)
I Spy Trees (and other *I Spy Books)* (Polystyle Publications)

Books for teacher reference

Looking Around in Town and Country Philip Sauvain (Franklin Watts)
Early Explorations Science 5/13 (Macdonald Educational)
The Seashore Alfred Leutscher (Franklin Watts)
Organizing School Journeys Michael Arkinstall (Ward Lock Educational)

Useful apparatus

Boards and pencils for outdoor writing; modelling clay; boxes for making models; plastic bags; cassette tape recorder; camera; measuring sticks or trundle wheels.

A purpose/resource grid

A purpose/resource grid can be used at the planning stage. It will indicate, at a glance, the books containing the information needed and other useful sources such as slides, film-strips and pictures.

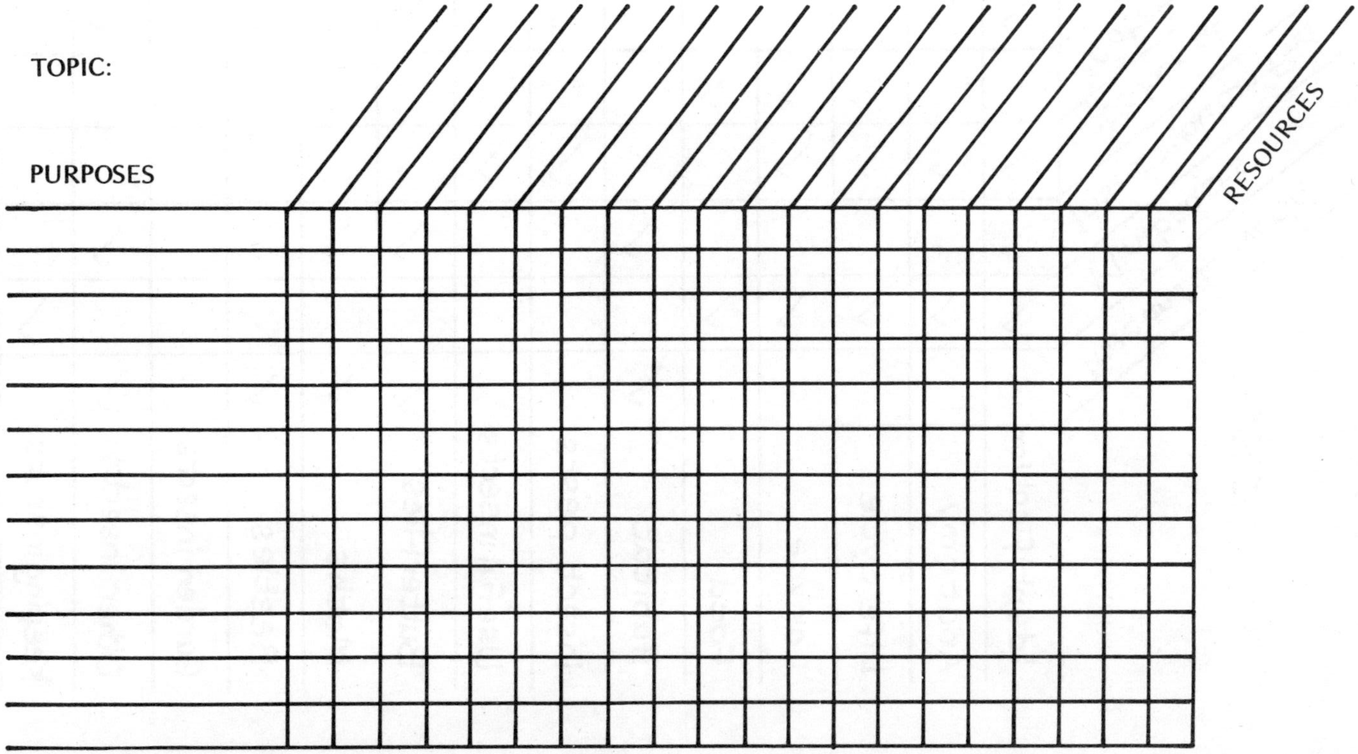

A completed purpose/resource grid

TOPIC: <u>Insects</u>

PURPOSES	Tree and its World	Minibeasts	Insects you can find	Let's look at Insects	Caterpillars	Insects	Bees	
Identification		✓	✓	✓		✓	✓	
Anatomy		✓		✓		✓	✓	
Life cycle		✓		✓	✓	✓	✓	
Larvae		✓		✓	✓			
Food		✓			✓	✓	✓	
Habitat	✓		✓				✓	
Insect pests				✓		✓		
Useful insects				✓		✓		
Butterflies	✓		✓			✓		
Moths	✓		✓			✓		
Beetles	✓		✓			✓		
Garden insects						✓		
Other insects	✓		✓			✓	✓	
Keeping insects		✓						

Oxford Book of Insects	Living Things	Ecology of Woodlands	Puffin – Gardening	Slides	Filmstrip	Pictures	Insects and other animals	RESOURCES
✓				✓	✓		✓	
							✓	
					✓	✓	✓	
✓					✓		✓	
✓							✓	
		✓	✓					
✓			✓		✓			
✓					✓			
✓		✓		✓	✓			
✓		✓		✓	✓			
✓		✓			✓			
✓			✓		✓	✓		
✓		✓	✓		✓			
							✓	

Books
Slides
Film Strip
Pictures

TEACHERS' REFERENCE BOOKS

Most of these have already been mentioned in the text, but they are all useful sources of information, and although specifically mentioned for use by the teacher, may have illustrations which could be used with the children.

ARKINSTALL, M. (1978) *Organizing School Journeys* Ward Lock Educational

BAINBRIDGE, J. W., STOCKDALE, R. W. and WASTNEDGE, E. R. (1970) *Junior Science Source Book* Collins

Book of the British Countryside (1973) Drive Publications for the Automobile Association

BURTON, J. (1968) *The Oxford Book of Insects* Oxford University Press

DEVON TRUST FOR NATURE CONSERVATION *School Projects in Natural History* Heinemann

Early Experiences (1972) Science 5/13 Macdonald Educational

Early Explorations (1974) Science 5/13 Macdonald Educational

JAMES, A. (1964) *Simple Science Experiments* Schofield and Sims

JARMAN, C. (1976) *Display and Presentation in Schools* A. and C. Black

JENNINGS, T. J. (1971) *Animals in the Home and Classroom* Pergamon

KEEN, D. H. and SIMMONS, G. E. (1976) *What on Earth Are We Doing?* Ladybird Books

LEUTSCHER, A. (1977) *The Ecology of Woodlands* Franklin Watts

MCCLINTOCK, D. M. and FITTER, R. S. R. (1976) *Pocket Guide to Wild Flowers* Collins

MACKEAN, D. G. (1973) *Introduction to Biology* John Murray

Minibeasts (1973) Science 5/13 Macdonald Educational

MITCHELL, A. (1974) *A Field Guide to the Trees of Britain and Northern Europe* Collins

NICHOLS, D. and COOKE, J. (1971) *The Oxford Book of Invertebrates* Oxford University Press

Ourselves (1973) Science 5/13 Macdonald Educational

SAUVAIN, P. (1975) *Looking Around in Town and Country* Franklin Watts

Science from Toys (1972) Science 5/13 Macdonald Educational

SHOWELL, R. (1972) *Looking at Insects and Small Animals* Ladybird Books

VAN DEN BRINK, F. H. (1978) *A Field Guide to the Mammals of Britain and Northern Europe* Collins

WHITE, A. (1968) *Geology for the Young Naturalist* A. and C. Black

WINDRIDGE, C. (1976/7) *General Science Books 1–5* Schofield & Sims

LIST OF SUPPLIERS

GENERAL APPARATUS

E. J. Arnold, Butterley Street, Leeds LS10 1AX

Animal cages
Binocular microscopes
Gardening and woodwork tools
Hand-lenses
Kaleidoscopes
Outdoor thermometers
Plastic measuring jugs
Plastic Meccano
Seconds timer

Osmiroid Educational, Osmiroid Works, Gosport, Hants

Balance with deep hopper pans
Hand-lenses
Lem magnifier (large lens on legs)
Pooter
Sand timers
Specimen boxes with magnifying lids
Unbreakable mirrors

Philip and Tacey Ltd, North Way, Andover, Hants

Measuring sticks
Plastic storage boxes
Rain measure
Timers

FILM-STRIPS AND SLIDES

Gateway Educational Media, St. Lawrence House, Broad Street, Bristol

Film-strips

Ladybird Books Ltd, P.O. Box 12, Beeches Road, Loughborough, Leicestershire LE11 2NQ

Film-strips (reproducing the illustrations from specific Ladybird books)

Visual Publications, 197 Kensington High Street, London W8 6BB

Film-strips and slides

Diana Wylie, 3 Park Road, London NW1 6XP

Film-strips and slides.

CHARTS

Macmillan Education, Houndmills, Basingstoke, Hants

Pictorial Charts Educational Trust, 27 Kirchen Road, London W13 OUD

Wallcharts

Philip and Tacey Ltd, Andover, Hants
Frederick Warne Ltd, 40 Bedford Square, London WC1B 3HE
Natural history wall pictures

SLIDE AND FILM PROJECTORS

Hanimex (UK) Ltd, Faraday Road, Dorcan, Swindon, Wilts
Hanimex Syllabus 4000 (slide/film-strip projector)
Hanimex Study-Vue (simple hand-viewer for slides and film-strips)

CASSETTE TAPE RECORDER

BASF, United Kingdom Ltd, Knightsbridge House,
197 Knightsbridge, London SW7 1SA
BASF 9110

Index